AMERICAN
MOLLY HOUSE

original screenplay by: Ryan Oeters

American Molly House exposes the sexual revolution in the times of the American Revolution through the eyes of multiple players with connections to the beginnings of the gay subculture in America. True to life stories of popular gay sexual identities, tricks of the 1770's underground tavern scene revealed and the explicit truths about the molly houses role in discovering the awakening in the eyes of best friends, libidinous sexual encounters, long term lovers, and victims of hate crimes. Insights into the fortunate of mankind and how important sexuality was to the 18th century American cause. Seymour and Morgans experiences in New York City with first time love, long term relationship and the rules of the game learned and taught by a sophisticated and intricate group of drinkers and card players. Drunken nights of rattle skulls and stonewalls evolving to private sexual fantasies fulfilled and fueled by attractive bartenders or movers, flashing signs for welcoming friends and customers upon interest. Slinky, young Tobias and Sebastians close relationship, tending a notorious hostelry and correspondence in Philadelphia's ring of elite including President Washington and some of his top men during the revolution. Gordons tale of vengeance in Providence portraying the harsh realities of 18th century hate crimes. Electric teens Zac and Jacobs titillating skills of the trade and triumphs tending a prominent Boston inn and pub financing their dream. Further exploration through stunning tales of late 18th century sexuality in America including slave and slave master relations, inviting teacher and apprentice encounters, sensuous scenes of caterwauling, a saucy saga about finding true family and romance along the way, the scandal of sodomites and the story of survival and success of the underground sex trade in colonial times portraying the American revolution's epics in style. Gallant, touching must see revelations, sharing anecdotes of the Americans fight for freedom with brilliant tales of sexual uniqueness and high spirits. The heavenly fate of six lustful players who unite in fashion retiring from the game together to a lavish estate on the coast. Sons of Liberty is proof arisen dreams really come true, finding independence and gaiety through amorous legends of brotherhood.

PRELUDE TO A REVOLUTION

Perched astutely inside a hale New York City tavern flirtatious, acute Thaddeus takes a liberal swallow from his cold beer. Quenching his early evening hankering, his curly golden mane hooks gazes as he tastes his lips and gives a swank smile to the suspired bartender.

BEST FRIEND KIBITZ

Slinky 18 year old Tobias carouses his rickety arms around his best friend Sebastian as they shine gaunt bodies with taut holds tussling in the towering olive green Philadelphia grass.

VIRILE VELOCITY

Lusty, electric teen Jacob hustling ensuing his ebony Australian Shepard Ash as she bustles across a Boston meadow. His mercurial buddy Zac succeeding convenient at his heels hotfooting to clip the beloved pet dog as they blitz through the ripe New England draft.

GORDY'S PRIDE

Butterball cheeked Gordon chaws jovially submerging into his titanic piece of cherry pie. Digesting his luscious prize on a dime and undeniably afore the line of four lardy finalists adjoining him on stage. Crumbs plunge off Gordons roly-poly chin slugging the outdoor stages timber mezzanine. The commingled crowd of elderly and juvenile eyewitnesses applaud while the contests rangy rawboned judge squeezes Gordons pudgy right forearm upraising it sky-high to the tittering horde.

JUDGE

Winner!

Gordon rumbles to lift his porcine beefcake from the peg pew as the swarm chants in piercing gay voices.

CROWD

Gordy! Gordy! Gordy! Gordy!

LASHED

The bald dark terra-cotta skin of Ceasar's African buttocks are exposed in equal parallel to the other defrocked slaves bound with canary rope tightly to wooden stakes. As Savannah slave owner Harry scourges him callously across his peeled cheeks while Ceasar wails in twinge as tears trickle from his flickering eyes.

APPRENTICE GRIND

Prominent blacksmiths son Gerard toiling abut a davenport in the basement workspace cloaks his rugged arms around the peaked chest of young apprentice Billy. Catechizing him how to hold the smoldering iron befittingly as Gerard sways Billy's hands in the proper lay enlightening him in midst lesson.

ROADSIDE ROBBERY

A chintzy teenage sonny is trooping along an empty Charleston street forlorn in the lurid South Carolina night. Suddenly a horse drawn buggy convoying two occult men approaches the gaudy boy and as he detours to face the buggy a pistol is weeded and clasped directly at him. The boy stops in his tracks realizing he is about to be robbed for the whole shebang he can give.

SPINNING TOPS

A cartel of lawless adolescents poised in a grand halo on a brick street in Raleigh. Gyrating tops for bets and snorting out loud. As the victor spinner collects his winnings in marbles and chocolate.

NAKED CLEANSING

The angelic sun setting over the Atlantic Ocean as the New Jersey coast is lambent. Statuesque 21 year old Morgan flings off his sark and trousers facing the indigo ocean water he ambers into the splintering waves and gambols into the Ocean relishing the ectasy of his stripped boody rasp in the cool water.

DRINKS ARE FREE

Strapping bartender Seymour with curtailed burnt sienna quills, matching perky brows and ultramarine eyes cocks in wake of the justled drinkery. Tilting a gorged crystal bottle of rum as he fills multiple cannikins to the top rim for the buoyed crowd of waiting macho patrons.

SEYMOUR

Rattle skulls are on the house, boys.

CLASSIC MOLLY

A privy door in the rear of a hostelry draws prudently behind two lasviscous young stripling as they fervidly begin to kiss mouths. Taking one anothers tunics off caressing their unrobed chests and fondle maws.

1770 PUNCHBOWL LIBERTY

8 anonymous hands each grasping a glass mug dunking them simultaneously into a colossal punchbowl filled with toddy. The bouquet of bountiful rum and nutmeg is skimming fresh in the air looping the men. Raising their impregnated mugs for a toast.

ANONYMOUS MAN

For the future of our sons shall liberty reign in New York and every colony.

Saluting mugs and slurping the toddy in united fashion the men exit the back doors of a shanty coupled to an auberge near city hall park in New York City. Carefully throttling a long wooden pole attached to the top an ensign with the single word "Liberty" on a royal blue conical cap. Carrying it discreetly in the bliss of the late night darkness without a word. Quickly surmounting the liberty pole resolutely in the ground hoisting it high in the night air staring up at its glory in sync. Giving a celebratory jig and slapping hands zestfully before scurrying wisely back to their safe house.

MANHATTAN DAYDREAMING

New York City, New York January 1770, a shipyard abreast the banks of the Hudson river. The auroral sun penetrates the early morning scene inside the crowded dockyard. Dockmaster Ryan stepping onto a capsized wooden crate waving both his hands ordering all his men to huddle around him. His burly 7 inch mahogany beard suspending his chins reach garnished with two light moss colored beads corkscrewed at the bottom attracts a legion of stares from the new guys. As the influx of crew form a circle beleaguering him, leaving an open space of 15 feet. The frayed grass and dirt spawn a slapdash arena anticipating to gaze a cock fight.

DOCKMASTER RYAN

Gents its time to introduce our dueling cock scrappers this morning. To my right last months champ Geronimo and his owner Davy.

Davy holding his senior cock with both hands firmly pageants Geronimo to the mobs kudos.

DOCKMASTER RYAN (CONT'D)

To my left virgin brawler Jupiter and his owner Jay. Let the bloodthirsty biddy's feud.

Jay steps forward tightly clutching Jupiter as he faces Davy. Simultaneously emancipating their cocks, immediately bombarding one another with careening blows. Jupiter remaining competitive in genesis but quavering to fatal scalping to Geronimos savvy at bouts omega.

CLOSE UP OF THE TWO COCKS BLOODIED FROM BATTLE

Hurrahs taper the crowd before the crew disperses to position

As twentyone year old Seymour is plodding with his hands bearing a keen ax. Standing six feet tall with a slender enduring build, his dishy coiffure resonates the suns sparkle. Flexing the meat on his triceps as he etches a great girder for a new skiff. Saturated with pristine sweat gobs across his forehead continuing to grind blinking his eyes to stymie the drips of sudor. His mind starts to spitball secretively. Morgan also 21 fit with rich beige hair flowing as he pivots his chopper next to Seymour. Morgan's avid physique for a shorter man of 5 foot 9 teamed with his sturdy daily yield had gained him a generous critique from Dockmaster Ryan.

SEYMOUR

I could sure use a fat bombo for my toil today.

As Seymour models his finesse revoking portions of a dream he had the night before envisaging a King somewhere on the other side of the world. The century and country is alien and seems to hint hundreds of years in the past. The Kings face limelights an intense energy as he spys a party of late teenage chaps dallying in the courtyard.

MORGAN

I'll be belting a stonewall when I wrap.

SEYMOUR

Let's deuce that plan.

Scudding profoundly into his daydream the King ordaining a serf to chaperon the shirtless lad he savored clowning in the quadrangle to his chambers. As the fancied boy is ushered inside he orders the serf to shut the doors behind him importuning the lad and king alone. Maturing his goad he focuses his sight on Morgans exposed forearms augmenting his glimpse to his treasure trail on his lower belly. In full blown reverie the King performs oral upon the acceding 18 year old boy to culmination. Succeeding ejaculation the king buffs his jowls white with his vestment and then stands up. Seymour watches closely as Morgan takes a pause and stares back at his fellow proletarian. Eyeballing that perseveres longer then a typical glance as they share a smile at one another for a twinkling. Seymour scans Morgans mouth cajoled by his appeal.

CLOSE UP OF MORGANS MOUTH AS HE SLOWLY LICKS HIS UPPER LIP FROM LEFT TO RIGHT THEN LOWER LIP FROM RIGHT TO LEFT

Edged by his air castle in the kings chambers he fathoms the king complasaintly imparting the boy to copulate in same fashion on him. Morgans bait charming him back to reality.

DISSOLVE TO:

THE SUN SETTING OVER THE HUDSON RIVER

The work day is finished and Morgan approaches Seymour while he is tramping away.

MORGAN

I see you possess mighty skills with your dirk, Seymour. Maybe you could give me a lesson sometime help me fine tune the speed of my strokes.

SEYMOUR

You did quite well today Morgan I must say with your hand and mine we may conquer this hull tomorrow. I tell you what if you like on Saturday you can give me company to this timberland I know of in the north. I pine to gather strong wood to build a spread to my flat I am scheming.

MORGAN

I fancy the opportunity Seymour. So you will meet me here Saturday and entertain my curiousity to your skill.

SEYMOUR

I welcome the chance, my friend. Let's plan for 9 right here and I'll take you to this ripe timberland.

FADE OUT.

PHILADELPHIA FANTASY

18 Year old Tobias donning angelic chestnut brown locks beetling his forehead and elapsing the seat of his ears escorts past his mother and father in avenue to his bedroom.

TOBIAS

After I finish helping you and pop in the field tomorrow I am going to the river with Sebastian to catch us some fish.

FATHER

Tobias you try hard to bring us home some superb tasting cod tomorrow. I will poach us a great dinner from your lasso the whole week. You can use the pot behind the house to keep em in. If you can do that for your pop, mom and Amelia I will bargain for a pair of modish chaps and chemise to wear to school.

TOBIAS

I'll do my best Pop sometimes those slimy things are hard to handle.

MOM

You will look so adorable for all the lassies in town with your dewy breeches Toby.

Overhearing her family talking from inside her room young lanky haired 14 year old Amelia peers at her brother.

AMELIA

Toby's hair is too shabby for him to find a girlfriend. Girls are supposed to grow the long hair. His face wont be pretty enough until I chop those crummy cowlicks for him.

TOBIAS

I can't trust no 14 year old mangling my hair. She'll end up cutting off my whole head. Maybe I'll let mom clip it but I have to think about it.

MOM

Go to sleep, there's oodles to do tomorrow, son.

TOBIAS

Good night Mom, good night Dad, night Amelia

As he shlepps the few remaining feet into the bantam free space in his living quarters in front of his bed. The muffled "good nights" from Amelia and his parents empty Tobias's ears. His parents enter their own room into privacy. Staring down at his bare feet Tobias gently tugs at his worn amber knickers and pulls them entirely off. Then yanks his white linen shirt overtop his head and tossing his clothes next to each other on a meager pulpit abutting his bed. Tobias standing a stark 5 foot 7 and winsome 120 pounds de facto bony physically he proudly peeks down at his unclad stomach. Rubbing his right hand crossing his belly button a few times he then raises his right arm up and flexes his bicep muscle to a crest.

CLOSE UP OF TOBIAS FLEXING HIS BICEP

Using his left hand to roll his fingers softly across his bulging brawn. Then scours his right hand through his bangs flinging them backwards over his forehead as he plops gaily down onto his bed. Laying uncovered for a breezy moment with his arms relaxed behind his head seemingly holding him up as if he had something peculiar on his mind. Reflecting on his day ahead of him and with a merciful snigger Tobias moves both his hands to his chalky underwear. Teasing his skin for a jiffy he eventually slides his underwear awry into glutted nudity. Enjoying the privacy of his bedroom alone and the crisp air around him he lays back this time with his hands resting on the upper part of his breadbasket. Looking up to the ceiling beginning to fantasize in his inherent world. First an image of Sebastian's athletic nature smiling at him the day before as the two best friends were leaving school together. Changing to his memory of sitting next to him at a desk during class as he goggles Sebastians hand write a note on a piece of paper using a pencil. He stares intently at how enchanting Sebastian's skin on his hand is as he brushes his cursive letters onto paper.

CLOSE UP OF SEBASTIAN'S HAND WRITING IN CURSIVE

Evolving to a memory of Sebastian poised outside his house with him shirtless. Reflecting past occasions that turned him on he continues his fantasy of Sebastian's dapper focusing in on his exposed nipple. Excitably gazing across his own chest and tight paunch. Lowering his right hand across himself slowly caressing in the first stages of calmy masturbating. Deepening his atlantis imagining Sebastian's teat becoming erect whilst reaching up squeezing his own right bust.

CLOSE UP OF SEBASTIAN'S DIVESTED CHEST AND THEN CLOSE UP OF HIS OWN NIPPLE AS IT HARDENS BEING SQUEEZED THEN LOWERING DOWN HIS STOMACH

Swapping remembering a time he and Sebastian were wrestling in the grass alone in an open field. Picturing Sebastian rolling on top of him and straddling him with his legs bent at the knees on both sides. Resting his butt easily on his solar plexus teasing him. Tobias progresses masturbating faster as he indulges in fantasia flush naked. His eyes shut as his pets increase stiffer and steadier.

CLOSE UP OF TOBIAS'S FACE AS HIS EYES ARE CLOSED SHOT MOVING SLOWING DOWN HIS ARM AS HE CONTINUES HIS JERKING MOTION

Shifting from him grappling in the barley to envisaging kissing Sebastian on his cushy lips. Seeing him fully encompassed in french kiss shared with his closest compatriot. Scoping himself tickling Sebastian's smooth body everywhere actualizing from his neck down his hardy chest and sleek arms, languiding coddling his navel. Converging to climax envisioning clinching below Sebastians waist spectacles him perfectly naked. Giving a posy his erection frenzies on his contracted abdomen. Sensibly giggling then sweeping his spout, eyes cling sealed.

CLOSE UP SEBASTIAN'S BULGE IN HIS BRITCHES SITTING AT THE WOODEN DESK IN CLASS TOBIAS LOOKS UP AND SEBASTIAN SURELY CATCHING HIM RUBBERNECKING WITH A GELASTIC LEER ON HIS FACE

TOBIAS TURNS TO SLANT AT THE TEACHER

Arouse dabbling in titillation for the next afternoon rendezvous with his favorite classmate he caps his torso with a wool blanket. Rolling to his right his mind fixes to armorous sleep state.

WHISKEY'S DESTINY

Zac trailing Jacob in chase of Ash as her stringy black bristles ebb wildly dashing in the ajar moorland. Halting to a breakneck corral of the dog around her chassis, Zac whacks hard into Jacobs dorsal knocking them both into a nestle. Laughing while they belly flop and Jacob rolls off the squatty share of Zacs body. Lollygagging forward to a kowtow as Zack hunkers up and slaps Jacob gingerly across his face.

ZAC

I can bag that bitch better than you any day.

JACOB

Were going to get so sponged tonight.

ZAC

You have to wake me up later just come to my window.

Jacob swats Zacs face back reciprocating and bucks to his feet.

JACOB

Don't be a wimp this time I'm taking you to see a ghost tonight and I got permission to gut the rest of the whiskey.

ZAC

Bring your rotgut we can bender I'll be on my bed

Jacob pirouettes and spasms after Ash as she beats his anchor on her.

JACOB

Later

FADE OUT.

A TASTE OF FREEDOM

4 hours blown Jacob ascends the window out of his room and races down the lane bisecting an airy tract into Zac's neighborhood. Tacitly prancing the crag paved drag solo then orbiting Zac's brick home. The rear window belonging to Zac is cracked sufficient for Jacob to cleave both hands under the posterior plucking up the skeleton enough for him to fit his torso inside. Frisking the walls with his palms Jacob coasts himself into Zacs room. Scanning him dozing even-steven with the cover and his debunked skin, seizes the blanket twirling it onto the floorboards. Slumbered nude Zac kindles but remains camped on his back scouting up at his friend.

ZAC

Your so early.

JACOB

Put some clothes on and lets push off.

ZAC

Where do you reckon your taking me I'm not getting in the river.

JACOB

Moonshine with me please.

Jacob passes Zac the brimming bottle of whiskey.

JACOB (CONT'D)

Were going to see the ghosts. We have to bounce the wall and find the best place. I'll tell you a story I know about, it's true.

ZACK

Who told you this ghost story I don't believe in ghosts your just drunk already.

Zac takes a slosh from the whiskey and retreating it to Jacob who supervenes with a swig. Zac pulling his slacks up and buttoning them. Cladding a milky pullover he rolls up his sleeves then pounces out the window mimicking Jacob onto the cobblestone. Strutting up a slighted hill and turning left following another lane. Approaching Copps Cemetery Zac and Jacob cumber the grey stone palisade. Zac cribs his hands to aid as a step while Jacob snatches the crown of the rampart pulling himself over then reaching for Zacs arms ballyhooing him to the other side. They tumble in blubbery grass inside the cemetery walls. Zac lets loose a coy laugh as Jacob quaffs the whiskey then handing it to Zac, who tosses and passes it back to his chummy rival.

JACOB

All the dead spirits in here know we are watching them.

ZAC

So tell me what exactly do ghosts do all day?

JACOB

Watch people. That's all they can do. Spy and wait for the perfect soul.

Jacob ushers Zac past the foreground along a dirt groove towards the apogee of the shadowy cemetery. Coming cold turkey to the facial of a grave marked Douglas Hoover and cooly slacken on the turf they perch contiguously. Swapping tastes from the jigger.

JACOB (CONT'D)

Its true when somebody jacks off alone atop a banshees grave, the spirit is bestowed the chance to possess their soul and re enter life again. Some spooks accept the coincidence and occupy fate. They call it being inside. Knowing they aren't their old selves anymore is obsessive that's why they like to haunt. Some deny nemesis and their door succumbs. Most hook except it rarely happens, getting off in a cemetery isn't always on a list of chores. That's why the acquainted spirits possess when it shakes.

ZAC

Your starting to scare me. I don't enjoy demons staring at me.

JACOB

It's legend the only manner they can steal your soul is if your alone jerking off. When you have a watcher with you while you do it destiny grants us the honor to give the ghost life or take them to the twilight.

ZAC

So who gets to be the watcher.

JACOB

We'll flip a marked stone. You call it in the air. Winner watches and loser jacks off first.

Marking the top of a nearby rock with a circle blotch of soil Jacob cast the stone up in the air.

SLOW MOTION OF THE MARKED STONE IN AIR

Zac calls circles before the stone lands circle up.

ZAC

So the watcher reserves the right to choose life of twilight.

Jacob promptly unbuttons his tan bloomers and lays back arising to masturbate rapidly in front of Zac. His erection being nourished tighter and unyielding as he is watched.

JACOB

If you enjoy a taste and swallow you open the door to salvation. Spit it and the spirit dies. Your choice. Jacob threatening orgasm as Zac bows beside him while his spritz splatters tenderly across Zac's schnozz and jaw. Licking neat his shaft then jacking up his head nabbing the jug swashing and filling his mouth to capacity. Swallowing as Jacob sits up and leans gently on Zac kissing him lazily. Zac in full tilt regurgitates the stomach full of whiskey on to Jacobs face and his own. Jacob scramming and rising to his feet tweaks on Zacs shoulder to cull him up with him then points to the far side of the cemetery.

JACOB (CONT'D)

Look that old man over there is screwing that's disgusting.

ZAC

That looks like Mr. Smith and that stupid kid from school. The really skinny short one.

JACOB

Let's get the hell out of here before that sick old man spots us.

As he leads Zac overtop the facade to the cobblestone on the other side.

ZAC

I can't believe we just saw that. I'm drunk and just saw the devil or Mr. Smith is so ugly.

JACOB

Next time you have to take me to a better place to get wasted.

Zac and Jacob dart down the street reappearing into their north end neighborhood.

FADE TO BLACK.

POUGHKEEPSIE ESCORTING

Hardy 23 year Thaddeus riding his sable stallion in panorama of the Hudson river departing Poughkeepsie, New York. His strawberry blond fluffs sway in the breeze as he espies a burgeoning lad walking alone near the banks. Slowing his stallion to a freeze abut the lad.

THADDEUS

May I ask where you are headed my friend perhaps I can be of avail.

Strutting forlorn in torn rags and carrying a bitty backpack straddling his shoulders.

JIMMY

New York sir, I am seeking a livelihood and a fine dame. These parts have yet to satisfy my longings.

THADDEUS

Hop on my colt, I can get us into the city in a chop chop and I sure could use the company for the ride. Jimmy hops up on the colt securing his arms around Thaddeus's chest as they take off briskly to the south.

JIMMY

My names Jimmy, yours? I am grateful for the escort, sir.

THADDEUS

I am Thaddeus and am headed to New York for a few days myself before trekking to Delaware to visit my brother. Maybe find a dandy boarding house to fix me a jezebel.

THE TWO RIDING THE STALLION ALONGSIDE THE HUDSON RIVER AS SUN SETS

Thaddeus ordering the stallion to halt by rivers edge. Him and Jimmy set up a makeshift fire as dawn concedes. Sharing the last remnants of Thaddeus's stash of turkey giblets and giving presumptuous stares before sniggles as they digest together. Suddenly a boisterous thunder resonates the sky around them and they both gambade onto the stallion and take off briskly in the darkness.

JIMMY

Anything I can do to be a worthy sojouner tonight.

THADDEUS

Just hold onto me tight and lets ride until we are spent.

Jimmy squeezes his arms around the middle portion of Thaddeus's abdomen for a juncture before slithering his hand pruriently around his jutting crotch masquerading a slip. Prolonging his coercion acknowledging the bloomer by glissading his hand around Thaddeus's raw dermis with corncupient tugs.

THE STALLION DASHING THROUGH THE DARKNESS AS THADDEUS ENJOYS JIMMY'S PHILANTHROPY

As a steady burst of rain embarks Thaddeus abruptly orders the stallion to a cessation and then him and Jimmy jump off, tying their horse sturdily to the corner of a near by barn before invading prudently. Plopping on some hay just inside the barn door together and immediately cosseting one another seducing to slumber.

THADDEUS (CONT'D)

We must wake before daybreak and decamp or they will hang us as heisters.

THADDEUS AND JIMMY NUZZLING IN THE HAY

FADE TO BLACK.

SATURDAY STROKING

FADE IN:

THE SUN RISING IN ORANGE AND PURPLE MORNING RAYS ABOVE MANHATTAN

Morgan stretches up as the sun casts through a window in his abode not far from the shipyard. Slipping into his trousers and ivory thread top, zealous to accost Seymour he takes a plentiful nip from a beaker of fresh milk. Soothing his throat before sauntering down the street, noticing a youngster racing across the artery. Amused at the youths pizzazz engaging his consorts Morgan enters the tavern and immediately notices Seymour sitting at a far end stool speaking to a bar hand. Approaching him he sits in the empty seat to his right and the bar hand lolls a cup of lukewarm coffee in front of him.

BAR HAND

Compliments of the White Rose any friend of Seymours is a friend of ours.

MORGAN

Thanks

BAR HAND

Enjoy

SEYMOUR

Well good morning Morgan you seem excited for your lesson today already.

Taking a drink from his coffee he cases Seymours face.

MORGAN

I am I just don't know what to expect.

SEYMOUR

Expect a perk from my advice, the dockmaster is seeking a few ace men to start on a trestle next week and asked me to help pick the best of the best to execute the task.

MORGAN

I can afford you benefit, So may I ask where are you bringing me today for this private coaching.

Coinciding sips from their coffee.

SEYMOUR

To a spot in the woods not many know of, its wholly wilderness and beautiful there. I espied rare timbers I want us to return today. There I will show you some things I was once shown myself that can advance your perspectives on stroking and wielding the hatchet the perfect way.

MORGAN

I shall wait to see for myself I presume this lesson will be enlightening and this cryptic grove you speak of seems daring.

SEYMOUR

Well lets head off Morgan I am ready to take you there.

As a suite of four bloke crow conspicuously they begin the first card game of the morning at the White Rose Tavern. The dealer distributes the cards out as Seymour and Morgan stand and promenade towards the front door. Kristopher the budding muscled dealer at the table fixes on Seymour as he crosses.

KRISTOPHER

Seymour will you be returning later for a game of six. I must introduce you to a mate I met the other day from an inn on 2nd.

SEYMOUR

Not today Christopher I have plans to teach Morgan a few things. I will take you up on that game tomorrow if you like.

KRISTOPHER

Okay then, I'll see you tomorrow for a match, go on.

As Kristopher and his gang forge ahead playing cards and Seymour and Morgan exit the White Rose onto the avenue. In unison leaping up into the carriage Seymour pilots the onyx horse in the direction of the coveted forest a ways north of the city.

FROM ABOVE THE CARRIAGE LOOKING IN THROUGH THE SIDE AS SEYMOUR AND MORGAN SIT NEXT TO EACH OTHER

Accessing the woodlands Seymour captains the horse along a modest aisle aside a brook. Enjoying silence and the scenery as the beat to the timbers augments to an elongated journey induced by Seymours memory of the once visited locale. He fixates on the edge of the creek and swelling medley of soaring spruce ahead.

SEYMOUR

Here we are Morgan I call this niche Mister Sister because these two hoary spruce sprouted so bold next to one another. The great one mister and his chief crony sister to his right.

Morgan peers high up to the tip tops of the giant pulps.

MORGAN

Beautiful in deed.

SEYMOUR

They shall be likewise stunning as my grand staircase, I gimmick to erect this year.

MORGAN

I fathom a noble project.

Jouncing from the carriage Seymour ties the horse tight to a tree and stands a hairs breadth to Morgan as they assay mister sister.

SEYMOUR

These stock are living lovers, sister and brother and have prized this forest for centuries. I will love stepping on them every evening to my bed.

Seymour snatches two chippers from a sack and hands one to Morgan.

MORGAN

This ax is much heavier than the ones at the shipyard.

SEYMOUR

It is, I was endowed these rippers from a wise man I met at the tavern last year. He brought me to his home and showed me his collection. He sharpened them to be used only for potent hardwoods. He explained the cutlass is unbreakable and with the impeccable stroke it takes half the time to conquer a valued plank then with a regular.

Seymour walks close to mister and clouts his right hand above his left veering at the bark with as much power as his body can throw. Morgan poising probing Seymours clamp as iotas of bark are slashed to the ground around them.

SEYMOUR (CONT'D)

See my grip Morgan. Come closer and stand behind me let me show you.

Morgan ambles behind Seymour gazing at both his hands clenching the core of the ax.

SEYMOUR (CONT'D)

Shoot your hands around mine.

Following order Morgan grasps his hands around Seymours right on top of right, left on left.

MORGAN

What's so special about this hold?

SEYMOUR

Let me show you just keep your hands on top of mine and I'll steer them the whole way.

Seymour yanks the ax banner back as far as possible and ripples into the cortex splintering more chunks. Pulling off from the blow and taking his right hand off the tomahawk handle moving his left hand upward in its place. Then replacing the lower spot with his right hand changing the positions of his hands from the last stroke. Morgans hands remain choked around Seymours, his chest flush on Seymours back. Both their legs spread steadfast to maintain a superior angle. Curving the next stroke with right hands below left hands and gouge into misters oblique. Morgan tightens fondle on the crank atop Seymours hams.

SEYMOUR (CONT'D)

This is called the change up. Just gives you more power changing hands between strokes.

MORGAN

Looks to be working so far.

SEYMOUR

We will finish mister together and then we can take turns on sister. Just keep your grip around mine and pay attention as much as you can to the push in my arms as we change up.

Smiling Morgan keeps his grasp tightly as they continue to chop hard and fast at mister. After every third swing Seymour would drop both his arms holding the ship axe down and rest them on the upper portions of his legs. The axe blade nestled on the ground for a few brief seconds then Seymour would lift the handle and begin the next successive swings. The second time Seymour rested his hands on his upper thigh area near his waist he turned his right hand outward forcing Morgans hand inward as it gently brushes up on his inner thigh near his groin. Leaving their hands resting for a few moments longer before the next three power strokes. Noticing how the back of his hands were brushing ever closer to Seymours crotch with each short rest not wanting to pull his hands off and say something he became somewhat stimulated and even excited as his hands touched Seymours body remembering his daydream the day before while working on the ship next to his friend. The next rest Morgan thinks he feels a hardening bulge rub against the back of his hands. Feeling a sense of closeness to Seymour he has never felt before or with any other male friend he liked this rush of adrenaline and noticing he was also becoming erect from inside his own worn trousers. Confused but stimulated sexually he thinks Seymour may be noticing a bump in his lower back area.

SIDE SHOT OF SEYMOUR AND MORGAN STANDING CLOSELY TOGETHER AND RUBBING PANTS

Maintaining his close hold around Seymours hands as they keep stroking away at mister reaching a highwater mark in the cut wood where it seemed the thick timber would fall at any moment Seymour remains completely quiet. Working hard and fast together both acknowledging the bulges and not stopping they stay focused on changing hands and stroking in the right tender spot. Finally one last impact conquers mister as the trunk snaps at the cutting point as they separate their bodies and hands for the first time in more then 10 minutes they back away and watch the tall tree crash beautifully to the forest floor.

SEYMOUR (CONT'D)

We did it.

MORGAN

That was fast.

SEYMOUR

I told you I would teach you something new today. Four hands is better then two but even using the change up alone cuts crisp and solid every time.

MORGAN

If we bring back all this wood on another trip your going to have enough to build your own church and become a pastor.

SEYMOUR

Can I ask you something Morgan. Do you think God brought you here today to help me chop down mister and sister for my new stairwell or do you believe there was an alternative destiny for you today.

MORGAN

Alternative destiny? Well I hadn't pondered one for today but I may say I am glad I came.

SEYMOUR

Morgan I want to give you a piece of my mind. They only way I can teach you the things I want to teach you is you let me do this for you now.

MORGAN

Do what?

Seymour walks close up to Morgan and looks kindly in his eyes and smiles.

SEYMOUR

You must close your eyes for me and please don't open them until I finish giving you the best part of your lesson today.

MORGAN

Alright if you think you can really teach me something.

Morgan shuts his eyes and waits to see what will happen next. Seymour chuckles briefly as he watches his friend obey his request then drops down to his knees. Reaching forward with both his hands he gently caresses Morgans bulge through his trousers. Surprised Morgan becomes immediately aroused by Seymours offer of affection. Deciding quickly in his mind to consent to Seymours actions as he slowly undoes his trousers and continues fondling his now almost full erection with both his hands. Rubbing his hands passionately up and down Morgans shaft and begins blowing him. Making sure to do his best to satisfy Morgan to completion he begins rubbing himself. Morgan keeping his eyes shut during then entire period of copulation pulling his head back to face the sky while he orgasms. Morgan savoring their first sexual experience opening his eyes and looking down at Seymour with a pacified grin Seymour stands up and before any words kisses Morgan on his lips. Encompassed and totally surprised by what has just happened Morgan is now relieved inside and feeling more love for anybody then he has ever before. Encompassing Seymour's soft lips while Seymour puts his hands around his arms and then pulling away.

SEYMOUR

Your very strong Morgan. I think you know now who I am and I am glad I think I know you better now too.

MORGAN

What do you want to know about me Seymour, Tell me?

SEYMOUR

I don't need to know any more then you want to share but what I can show you next can change your life forever.

MORGAN

Show me?

Seymour pulls off his shirt and tosses it to the ground now standing bare chested and again looking into Morgans eyes.

SEYMOUR

The next thing I can show you is something you can't see here in this forest. It's bigger then you and I, but you are now awakened and you must be taught all the rules of the game.

MORGAN

Awakened to what?

Seymour starts to take off his trousers and now stands totally nude as he picks up the axe and walks over towards the second now lone standing tree.

SEYMOUR

Awakened to the game.

As he swings his naked body hard at sister chopping the first bite into the bark. Then continuing with his next stroke. Morgan standing with his trousers still unbottoned watching Seymour chop away at sister naked he has a feeling he has never cultivated before. Curiosity fills his stomach and seems to jolt up through his chest and into his face as Seymour swings away at sister. His nude body showing no signs of struggle or hesitation between strokes Morgan keeps his eyes on him as he begins to walk closer.

MORGAN

You speak of a game but where are the players?

Seymour pauses and again chuckles at Morgans statement. Resting the axe head on the ground and turning to face his friend.

SEYMOUR

I will show you but not now. We must wait until Wednesday night. I will take you there then and let you see for yourself. The rules are simple and benefits are great. The only thing I ask of you is for your secrecy. From today forward everything I tell you must be kept as a lesson from god for you to know and not to speak about to anyone.

MORGAN

I have not heard word of any such enlightenment before? I am curious to see what this is all about so I will keep your secret.

SEYMOUR

I will trust you with the truth when you know all of it. Everyone who learns the game respects the game and everyone who plays. Never does anyone lose dignity and privacy is essential. On Wednesday night follow me after work to a pub I know of. There things can happen for you Morgan. Good things that will prove your manhood and a brand new opportunity you shall cream from everyday from here on forward.

MORGAN

Sounds like you got a plan for me, well its your lucky day because I was going to ask you for advice to find the best drink in town.

SEYMOUR

We are going to have that drink together when we meet next. Keep your patience there is more to learn. Just promise me this is between us only and we can sleep better the next few nights waiting.

MORGAN

I promise.

Seymour keeps chopping at sister as bark flys off the wounded tree to the ground. Morgan offers to help him finish and grabs the axe from Seymour and starts stroking hard and fast into the groove. Practicing the change up technique used on mister sister falls in half the time. Morgan and Seymour celebrate with a laugh as sister lands on the plush green grass.

FROM CLOSE UP OF SEYMOUR AND MORGAN LAUGHING AT THE CHOPPED TREE ROAMING FURTHER AWAY AND THEN UP ABOVE THE TALL TREES OF THE FOREST IN BRIGHT DAYLIGHT INTO THE SUN.

FADE OUT.

BEST FRIENDS FOREVER

THE SKYLINE OF 1770 PHILADELPHIA MOVING OUTWARD TOWARDS THE BANKS OF THE SKUHLKILL RIVER.

Able-bodied 18 year old Sebastian with his majestic 6 foot and 130 lb. svelte build is rollicking on boulders by the rivers threshold. Strutting across a bundle of broad close knit rocks jutting the rivers edge, suddenly a yell from a top a near by hill catches his attention recoqnizing the young patois as Tobias he looks over. Tobias hotfooting agilely down the hill to catch up with Sebastian at the riverbank. Reaching the waters hem and his confidant still poised a top an avant-garde stone he laughs out loud.

TOBIAS

Your going to fall and drench yourself.

SEBASTIAN

How about I give you a drenching.

As he leaps to the muddy banks of the river landing on both feet and grabbing a hold of a smaller Tobias with both arms. Teasing him with a bear hug acting as if he is going to pick him up and fling him into the river.

TOBIAS

I can't swim I will drowned.

SEBASTIAN

You mean I have to teach you how to swim and fish today, what good are your parents.

TOBIAS

I don't need my parents anymore I swear. I don't need school either I can take care of myself for the rest of my life.

SEBASTIAN

The rest of your life isn't going to be very long if you can't swim.

As he whammies Tobias by bunny hopping him into the water. A solid jolt that thumps him off balance while he tumbles face forward into the surging river. Going under for a jiffy then pulling his head above water, Sebastian cackles hysterically then lurches in after his schoolmate. Alighting next to him dabbling in the nippy water he goads Tobias and douses his head under letting him up for air and then spraying his face with a hand full of river water. Tobias getting high on the harassment spattering a volley of river water back at Sebastians bewitched face.

SEBASTIAN (CONT'D)

My pop told me once if you want to catch the fish you must understand them first. Getting in the water with them is like sharing their bed. We just have to catch them while they are sleeping.

Continuing to wade in the river a few minutes then lifting their deluged clothed bodies out standing next to each other on the shore snorting.

TOBIAS

I got to let my clothes dry off before I go home.

As he rips of his wet shirt and drops it on a near by grassy area then takes off his shoes and sits them next to his shirt. Sebastian follows resting his shirt and shoes next to Tobias's.

SEBASTIAN

Are you scared to get naked in front of me?

Sebastian wriggles off his underwear and plops them next to his shirt standing wholly nude in front of Tobias. He laughs unabashedly and smiles before turning and jumping back into the river going under for a moment then surfacing. Tobias snickering at his friend wiggles down his dank underwear and sets them next to the soaked clothes to dry then pounces into the river naked following Sebastian.

Wallowing water at each others faces as suddenly Sebastian freezes and shams a surprised look at Tobias before tugging both his hands underwater.

SEBASTIAN (CONT'D)

Something is grabbing me, it has a hold of me.

Relinquishing a shrill before his head vanishes underwater.

TOBIAS

Sebastian!

Tobias shrieks out staring acrose the river looking for Sebastian to emerge.

UNDERWATER SEBASTIAN SWIMS TOWARDS TOBIAS'S NAKED BODY AND THEN REACHES FORWARD WITH BOTH HANDS GRABBING HIS RIGHT FOOT AND YANKING HIM BENEATH. SQUEEZING AROUND HIS CHEST FROM BEHIND HIM AS THEY ARISE SIMULTANEOUSLY.

TOBIAS (CONT'D)

What are you doing to me?

SEBASTIAN

Saving you from the hellion river gnomes in these waters. One just dragged me under trying to take me to the incubus's realm.

TOBIAS

Do you really believe in hobgoblins? Why are you holding me?

Sebastian keeps his arms around Tobias gripping him tightly with his head behind Tobias's speaking to him vigilantly.

SEBASTIAN

The story has it the incubuses can only bite one person at a time. They are known to swim this river controlling fish bodies with their lost soul.

TOBIAS

Who's lost soul?

SEBASTIAN

The lost souls of the unlucky ones who died in this river. The legend goes that after their untimely death when a person drowns in these waters the incubuses steal their light. Then they breed like vampires swimming for eternity searching for lonesome victims entering their underwater realm.

TOBIAS

You are just joking right, you aren't serious are you?

SEBASTIAN

I wouldn't lie to you I don't want us to die. There have been true cases once bitten from an incubus fish the infected person begins to lose their own mind. It takes time but eventually you become a succubus.

TOBIAS

I would suppose we don't get bit then.

SEBASTIAN

We must stay together or the fiend that snagged me will try again.

With both their bare skin rubbing underwater and Sebastians arms wrapped sublimely becoming enchanted a rapturous pinch saturates Tobias's as he turns his face towards Sebastian smirking.

TOBIAS

Your bluffing about the legend aren't you.

SEBASTIAN

Legends don't lie but friends will at times. I have something to tell you but first I want to know that I can trust you. Secrets only stay with best friends. Can I think of you as a best friend or only just a good friend.

TOBIAS

I'm your bestest best friend ever trust me I won't tell your secret to anyone, what is it?

SEBASTIAN

Paul was my last best friend and he moved away a few months ago and our secret stayed with us. Paul was the one who showed me how to tend the pub on weekends but he lives up in Massachusetts now. I know lots of guys at school who are friends but all they do is lie to look good. Best friends can do more then just look good. Paul taught me that having a best friend can be better then just a boring girlfriend.

TOBIAS

I don't even have a girlfriend right now.

SEBASTIAN

I know that but that doesn't mean best friends can't do everything a girlfriend can do.

TOBIAS

So that's your secret.

SEBASTIAN

Yes

TOBIAS

Are you going to show me how?

As they gander each others sopping faces eminently.

SEBASTIAN

Rule number one is after admitting best friends can't lie they must prove who has the bigger prick and he gets the licking first.

TOBIAS

Who judges?

SEBASTIAN

We do.

Sebastian liberates Tobias from his clasp and they make their way to the edge their naked bodies trickling with water chortling as they scope unclad physiques. Sebastian belly ups to Tobias smack dab while he bursts hysterically albeit his best friend.

SEBASTIAN (CONT'D)

Calm down and look at me in my eyes. Rule number two is everything from now on must be our secret. Nobody can know about us ever best friends must trust each other always. Do you promise?

TOBIAS

I promise.

Sebastian rivets profoundly into Tobias's eyes then kisses him quickly touching his hand over Tobias's as they penetrate their shafts sedately. Cuddly and in sync arousing erections carresibly to gauge goods.

LOOKING DOWN FROM EYE LEVEL HANDS BUFF SIZING SHAFTS

Poised mirroring the moment Sebastian dawns a second kiss Tobias echos in wistful muse.

A FISH SWIMMING BY IN THE RIVER AS HIS PUPILS DILATE.

FADE TO BLACK.

AFTER THE GAME - MARCH 5TH 1770

Playing futbol in an open grassy mead the covey of stripped chested teenage boys kick the round khaki ball back and forth passing it between them fighting to position for a goal. As a boy streaks down the side and breaks free from the nearest to him kicking the ball ahead fiercely into the makeshift goal marked by wooden barrels. Jumping up to celebrate the score his teammates yell and run to catch up. The ball continuing to roll further past the edge of the goal coming to a stop at the feet of three elder lads as they approach the game. Scott who bores shoulder length blond locks and heckled stare walks onto the field with two chums Robert and Samuel. The three 21 year olds are visibly drunk as Scott picks up the ball and carries it with him. The three friends approach the younger boys still laughing and slapping each other after the winning shot. 16 year old bony faced Cuddy who scored the goal has his back turned to his brother Scott while he is struck with the ball thrown in the middle of his back knocking his scrawny body to his knees.

SCOTT

Games not over, stupid.

As Cuddy turns around to face his brother.

CUDDY

Think your funny don't ya. Looks like you are outnumbered, dummy.

Cuddy motions for his two closest friends Jacob and Zack to lead him and the rest of their buddies in an attack running at Scott, Robert and Samuel. Altogether ten boys 16, 17 and 18 sprint towards them tackling each of them to the ground while they give a resilient rumble back. Successfully pushing off the first couple younger boys but quickly trampled by the bevy.

SCOTT

Will you jack asses get off me and come get drunk with us.

ROBERT

Why do you think we came to see you fools. Were too old for futbol and so are all of you. It's time for you all to start drinking with the big boys.

CUDDY

The big boys, eh.

SAMUEL

You all got to learn how to drink with the big boys before you can be a real man.

ZAC

So if we come drinking with you dicks does that mean we get to sit with the peachy dames at your place.

SCOTT

We are going to teach you boys to hold down some liquor first then show you where the real tramps hide.

Cuddy lets his older brother up off the ground as the other boys follow allowing Robert and Samuel to stagger to their feet.

CUDDY

Cmon' we don't got anything better to do today.

Motioning to his buddies to follow his brother.

JACOB

Who all wants to come with Cuddy's brother?

Looking at the rest of his futbol buddies as they smile at him pondering their decision.

ZAC

I'll come.

Three other boys Eben, Jack, and Charles agree to cortege Cuddy, Jacob, and Zac as they gait towards them while the four others deny the offer explaining they have to be home for lunch.

SAME DAY MASSACRE

Outside the customs house on King Street in downtown Boston apprentice wigmaker Edward Garrick calls out to British Soldier John Goldfinch as he leaves in complaint he has not paid a bill due to his master. Private Hugh White the soldier on duty reacts to the boys claim, challenges him and strikes him on the side of the head with his musket. As Garrick cries in pain fellow companion Bartholomew Broaders starts to argue with White as a large troupe of civilians begin to form around the scene.

NEARBY CIVILIANS FASTLY CLOSE IN SURROUNDING THE SCENE

DISSOLVE TO:

HUNG PROVEN

Scott squires the six junior cronies through the open cropland into a wooded area and to the breadth behind a humble shanty, Scott and his allies had built and which had obviously been used as a hang out. Walking up to a copious rectangular lectern set up with a bench seat braced against the posterior of the shanty, further wooden chairs surrounding the three other sides. Vast glass bottles filled with various rum, whiskey and gin with crystal tasters arraying the table. Scott grabs a cruet laden with rum and pours each of the boys their first drink. Robert and Samuel hand them out so they can start sipping.

SCOTT

You won't taste a better rum in the navy. This stuff will light you boys up.

EBEN

I'm going to join the navy next week.

JACK

I'd get so sick out on a ship all day with no lasses around.

They all sip their rum.

CHARLES

I've heard some butch ladies pose as men to enter the navy just so they can coition with all the crew.

CUDDY

Yea I have heard that too but the men find out and allow it, taking turns on the floozies.

JACOB

I bet the officers don't mind either and use those bimbos for their own ration.

ZAC

Maybe while their at sea but when they get inland they get a lashing and booted forever I'm certain.

As the six confreres finish their first cup of rum simultaneously.

SCOTT

You boys need to drink yourselves more rum or we'll give you a lashing.

Robert ante ups their second replete cup of rum with a chortle as they take swigs smirking at each other.

JACK

So where are these places you know of to find us these hot tootsies?

SAMUEL

You all must prove to us your a big boy before we share our secrets.

Jack wolfs his second libation while the others continue with their gulps. Setting it on the table steadfastly as Robert fills it again. He then stands up loyally on his chair and unravels his trousers in front of everyone.

JACK

My boy isn't just big. My big boy is huge.

As he pomps his colossal penis expoing it's grandeur to evince his compatriots, as an onrush of sniggering parrots the air. Fingers point at Jack poised on the chair wielding his pole flitting it back and forth with swagger.

EBAN

Damn that thing is a monster.

CHARLES

You gonna find yourself a fine doxy to squeeze you out a village with that someday.

JACK

I am going to have myself a huge family all because of my humongous rod. So is this enough proof for you.

CUDDY

That's enough elephant boy.

Jack tightens his trousers back up and steps off the chair grabbing his third drink and sloshing it with the others.

SCOTT

That just proves one of you who has a big dong but the rest of you fellows aren't verified.

Samuel rests his right elbow on the table and motions for Eben to grab his hand and arm wrestle with him.

SAMUEL

Come on Eben if you think your strong enough to join the navy then you can finish your drink and try to beat me.

Holding his glass to his mouth and downing the remaining rum Eben doesn't hesitate and reaches his elbow on the table scrunching Samuels hand. Robert grips the top of their hands and counts down.

ROBERT

3,2,1.

Samuel and Eban commence their arm wrestling match as everyone watches with gusto guzzling their rum. The contest starts evenly but after a few moments Samuel starts to overpower Eban as his arm lowers towards the table in defeat. Trying to hold up he maintains gaining some leverage back but then loses it again and struggles longer to prevent losing to Samuel. Finally Samuel slams Eban's fist to the table winning the bout and separating hands.

SAMUEL

Maybe after you get out of the Navy you'll be stronger kid.

Robert bashes his elbow to the table and looks at Charles challenging him to a match. Happy to accept Charles squeezes Roberts hand, Scott holds the top of their hands and counts down.

SCOTT

3,2,1.

Charles begins the match by overpowering Robert. Roberts hand goes all the way down about two inches from losing and almost slamming against the table as he holds his ground for a few moments.

ROBERT

I'm not that easy son, just testing you.

As he begins to gain ground and leveling out as their hands are throttling one another tightly while the others root them on. Then Robert begins to push Charles hand back surprising him with his sudden burst of power, then slamming his fist down in victory and letting go.

CHARLES

I thought I had you.

ROBERT

Well maybe after a few more drinks you'll do better.

Charles laughs and looks at his hand slightly reddened and sore.

EBAN

Sorry fellows but we oughta head back if we want to catch us all some eating before dark. We still got a good walk home.

SCOTT

Leaving so soon. Next time we'll have some gin and whiskey for you all and some more ways to prove yourselves.

ROBERT

I'd watch your back in those woods after drinking. There are true stories about crazy drunkards stumbling this way. They can smell some good rum a mile away and will come after you all mistaking you for a pretty lady.

RUM RHAPSODY

EBAN

We can handle the woods I'm not scared of any old man.

JACK

Let's go I'm so starving.

As he leads Eban and Charles away from the table towards the woods the way they entered. Cuddy stands and starts to follow them.

CUDDY

You guys can stay longer and drink with my brother me and Eban caught the fish his father is cooking up for supper I want to taste it.

SCOTT

They'll be fine we will to teach them how real men drink tonight. We have the best rum in Boston to share with you lucky bastards.

ZAC

We'll meet you at the docks tomorrow.

CUDDY

Alright.

As he follows Jack, Eban and Charles deeper into the woods and out of sight. Samuel hands Jacob and Zac the next full cruet of rum.

FADE OUT.

FROM A RIOT TO A REVOLUTION

As a feisty crowd of at first 50 Bostonians grows to 300 to 400 surrounding the area near the steps of the customs house. Runners alerted the barracks as a syndicate of officers with loaded muskets arrived to relieve White who was being insulted by the crowd. Snowballs and rocks are thrown at the officers daring them to fire as they continue to intimidate the British soldiers in swelling numbers. Abruptly a thrown object strikes an officer and knocks him down to the ground and his musket out of his hands. Angrily he gets up and yells to fire. Commanding Officer Preston does not give the order to fire but in a matter of seconds a series of ragged shots ring out into the crowd. Dispersed and striking eleven civilians. Hitting servant Crispus Attucks and killing him instantly the paniced crowd reacts violently and flees for protection.

EIGHT SOLDIERS POINTING THEIR MUSKETS AT THE CROWD AS THEY FLEE

Seventeen year old apprentice Samuel Maverick lays on the bricks near by suffering from a fatal wound bleeding profusely.

CLOSE UP OF BLOOD DRIPPING OFF HIS HEAD ONTO THE BRICKS

FADE TO RED.

DRINKING LESSONS

Scott clasps his hand around the bottom of a cruet as he guides it emptying into Zac's mouth. Robert doing the same with Jacob's as they both finish and lick their lips. Looking at each other Zac and Jacob becoming indubitably drunk smile for a moment when they make eye contact and then turn to face Scott, Robert, and Samuel relaxing next to them at the table.

SCOTT

So tell me when is the last time you boys had a damsel please you.

Laughing out loud undoubtedly more caroused by the passing seconds.

JACOB

There isn't a damsel in this town who can handle my schlong.

He chuckles while Samuel devours his brew and fills more rum.

ROBERT

So that means you must let Zac handle it for you then.

SAMUEL

Zac's a big man now he's had a lot to slug. I bet he is good at handling heavy loads for his best friend.

Zac reaches over and pushes Jacob's taut stomach teasing him.

ZAC

Jakes the one with the more girly voice. Look at his lips I don't think they get that red just from kissing his girlfriend.

Samuel clouts the replenished cup to Jacobs lips forcing the rum down his throat again. Swallowing and shutting his glazed eyes while his mind melts into a drunken stupor.

FADE OUT.

APOTHECARIES MASTERPLAN

A fresh painted sign on the front door of his offices in the outskirts of downtown Jamestown, Virginia reads Matthews Apothecary. The crisp letters alerting patients to his sacred abode he also calls home on the second floor above the lobby. All four walls are lined with shelves of colored vials of all sizes, most with tags representing their healing purposes. Various objects used for therapy and for the many patients he sees every working day lay in the room miscellany. His 17 year old practicing apprentice Calvin standing 6 ft. 4 with lanky thin arms and legs matching his beanpole build looks astutely at Dr. Matthews while he pours a green bottle of syrup used for healing headaches into a larger brown bottle. Calvin holding the brown bottle for his teacher while he spills syrup.

DR.MATTHEWS

You know I told your father the other day how fast a learner you are and that I think you will be a great doctor someday Calvin. I've noticed how bright you are son and how well you work with those strong hands of yours.

56 year old Dr. Matthews maintaining perfect health, well shaped body and smooth clean shaven face to keep his respected image as the top Apothecary in Jamestown. He concludes pouring the syrup and stares into Calvins hazel eyes.

CALVIN

Thanks, Dr. Matthews you know I would never leave this job even if I was asked to lead an army. Medicine is my life.

DR. MATTHEWS

Calvin I want you to sample this fine syrup for your doc. It will help greatly to rid you of any headaches and your sleep will improve. You can always brag to our patients how good it works, shall you have a taste?

Dr. Matthews reaches behind him grabbing a cup from a shelf and filling it to the top with bronze syrup then handing it to Calvin, who happily obliges lifting the cup to his mouth digesting the medicine then playfully rubbing his stomach. Within just three winks he experiences light headedness spinning into full blow dizziness before entirely losing consciousness and falling towards Dr. Matthews, catching Calvins fall with both hands. Discreetly dragging his limp body into a room in the back and resting him gingerly on a bed. Laying Calvins hands back behind his head then standing above him smiling to himself.

FADE OUT.

DREAMING THE BEGINNING

CLOSE UP OF JACOBS EYES OPENING BRIEFLY THEN SHUTTING AGAIN

As he is arranged on his back on a bed inside the shanty too drunk to know what is happening. A bright light is twinkling in his eyes as his loaded state of half consciousness is teasing him. Shirtless and reeking of rum both his hands are tied softly behind him to the bed posts. Both his feet are similarly tied to the other end of the bed. Zac is reposed on a bed next to him also shirtless and only wearing his underwear. He is not tied to his bed but is sleeping, beyond looped off so much rum and not aware of everything taking place around him. Scott and Robert stand near his head watching his face as his eyes slowly open and close in bewilderment. Samuel postured on the bed in between Jacobs spread legs giving him a blowjob endeavoring him to copulate and fancy the hot drunken experience to its maximum. As Jacobs erection stiffens and appears burning close to orgasm he opens his eyes and keeps them open seemingly noticing Robert and Scott staring down at him smiling and thumbing his cheeks. Scott slides his finger inside Jacobs mouth chinking it wide while he peaks with Samuels help. Robert caressing himself over his pants for a jiff while he watches and then walks over to Zac and slowly ties his hands and feet to the bed posts. Scott taking his finger gently out of Jacob's mouth.

SCOTT

This is a normal night of drinking for us real men Jacob. The lucky ones we invite to party with us like you boys tonight are all free to choose to be however you want to be. This is all just our way of showing you the better life.

SAMUEL

It's our way of bringing you closer to heaven.

ROBERT

Only the righteous boys survive their first night with us. We have many close friends we party with here at times Jacob. This is only one our places we come to get together. We rendezvous with many other boys like you two and in many other places.

SCOTT

When you and Zac wake up in the morning from your dreams. If you remember what happened tonight you are both welcome to join us anytime. We want to see you both more and of course that means you've chosen to accept our god. You will get to shindig with all the others. We entertain and host only the cool and best who understand our god and the benefits are forever.

Robert performs oral sex on Zac, instantly thrilled he opens his eyes lifting his head to look down to witness Roberts affection. Not saying anything and conceding Robert to continue he watches a few seconds longer then lays his head back in indulgence. Scott unties Jacob's hands and Samuel undoes his feet ballyhooing him up roving him the few feet over to Zac's bed. Settling him smoothly next to Zac but not tying him up. Scott then unties Zacs hands and Samuel undoes his feet while Robert pleasures him as Jacob watches curiously in euphoria resting next to him on the same bed. Scott initiates to rub Jacobs upper thigh with his hand then reaching forward toward his neck pulling him lower towards Robert's head as he is sucking his best friend.

SCOTT (CONT'D)

Show Zac your having fun tonight.

After waking from his drunken swoon, wholly absorbed in his libertine curiosity and in lustful crave Jacob starts to blow Zac as Robert moves closer to Zacs face. Zac glances down again briefly noticing his best friends face in place of Roberts. Enraptured with the satyric moment his heart chirrups amorously by the rum induced sensations conquering his thoughts.

SAMUEL

Why don't you show Jacob how much you like him back.

Zac with no objection prevails to suck Jacob at the same time. Scott, Robert and Samuel galvanized by espying the buzzed best friends 69 in front of them. Robert begins to kiss Samuel as Scott stands encompassed by the beauty of the scene slowly does a shimmy watching closely then pauses to fill two cups for one last drink. Jacob and Zac passionately culminate and lay back next to each other to relax. Both deeply intoxicated and royally perked by one another Scott holds up a cup to each of their mouths. Abetting them to swallow the last of the rum which will briskly conk them for the night.

SCOTT

This is a safe house boys. There's nothing to worry about waking up here. Just remember dreams are only dreams its up to you to believe in them or not.

SAMUEL

There's much more we can show you boys. There will always be a place to spree with us again another time, we promise.

ROBERT

Sleep well.

Scott blows out the lit lamp near by after noticing both their eyes flickering and shut as they lay slumbered abut each other on the same bed. Covering them with an indigo wool blanket before he, Samuel and Robert leave the shanty into the darkness of the hours past midnight.

FADE TO BLACK.

A DOCTORS DREAM

Dr. Matthews dozed on the bed fixedly cuddled up against Calvins body catnapped and bare chested, his left arm covering Calvins torso. He remains asleep for a few seconds before arising and staring up at Calvins face paying attention to his closed eyes. Raising and kissing Calvin on the cheek then grasping his white linen shirt off the floor and sliding his sleeves over his arms and around his rib cage. He then exits his office promenading to Calvins parents home a few blocks away alerting them their son is asleep in the office explaining he will be dandy when he wakes that there will be no lingering effects to his oversleeping. Respecting Dr. Matthews opinions concerning his passed out apprentice son the two adults walk to the office and then carry Calvins static body back home patronizing him serially into bed.

DR. MATTHEWS

I apologize for the inconvenience this evening sir, please tell Calvin to take a couple days off and come see me as soon as he feels well again.

CALVINS FATHER

I will do that Dr. Matthews, thanks for your help, have a good night.

Dr. Matthews glances at Calvins numb body and then at his father before leaving his apprentices home back to his office.

FADE TO BLACK.

PROVIDENCE RISING

FROM HIGH ABOVE THE CITY LIMITS OF 1770 PROVIDENCE RHODE ISLAND ZOOMING DOWN INTO A SCHOOL YARD FULL OF STUDENTS EXITING THE SCHOOL AND STANDING CONVERSING NEAR BY

A posse of friends in brown trousers and white school shirts exit the school walking adjacent each other across the open school yard mustered with other students as the school day has just concluded and the sun is shining above. Sitting in the glistening grass near a petty stone fence bordering the school yard from the street near by is Gordon, with his worn mahogany trousers and hoary school shirt snug around his protuding belly. The bottom of his shirt is loose exposing his bare skin from belly button down while he snacks on a green apple minding his own business quietly. Nicholas and Stephen, ring leaders of their posse approach Gordon resting his back up against the stone fence biting into the apple.

NICHOLAS

Hey fat ass can't your mommy afford you a bigger shirt. That's a gross display of affection you have for your ugly tummy. The girls around here don't need to see such a thing tubby.

STEPHEN

Can't you teach yourself to quit grubbing so much tubby. One day we are all going to have to roll your chubby ass down to the ocean and hope you float back to England where you belong.

Four badgering friends stand behind Nicholas and Stephen pointing at Gordon as the tallest in the group Peter throws a small rock at his bald stomach as it bounces off and falls to the ground.

GORDON

That hurt you bastard if you don't leave me alone I'm going to get Mrs. Frank and you'll be in trouble for bugging me.

PETER

Did you just call me a buggerer you stupid fat homo. Your too heavy to even think straight aren't you faggot.

NICHOLAS

You are staring at Peter's crotch aren't you. We all know you won't ever get a girl in this lifetime blubby. Dream on because if we catch you staring at any of our crotches again you won't have one of your own to take your next piss.

GORDON

Please leave me alone you creep

Stephen reacts by combatively grabbing the apple out of Gordons hand by his mouth and yanks a pencil from his pocket. Clenching the apple in front of him he stabs it riotously with the pencil.

STEPHEN

You best pretend you didn't call Nick a creep because next time this sick apple is going to be your fat ass and my pencil is going to be a hell of lot sharper. You talk back to us again and we are going to teach your humongous ass a lesson.

GORDON

I didn't do anything to you guys, why me?

NICHOLAS

Because your so fat you dumb shit. Christ won't accept people your size into heaven.

GORDON

People of God come in all sizes.

PETER

Well your wrong because your singing Satans song with every meal you finish. You might have time to work it off before you die or you might not.

STEPHEN

Gordon doesn't look that smart. I've seen plenty of fat people with big houses and good lives but not as fat as Gordon. If you don't stop eating Gordy your going to break the pillory before they hang you for obesity.

GORDON

Will you guys please leave me alone.

NICHOLAS

You don't want to be left alone to eat yourself all the way to hell, now do you Gordy. It's always better to have friends help you get there faster.

As he signals his friends to grab Gordons arms and they surround him from both sides taking two of them for each of his flabby arms. Squirming and trying to fight them off Gordon spits at Nicholas while his buddies hold his arms up above his head unable to move sitting on the grass. Peter pulls up the rest of his shirt above his chest to his neck. Nicholas reaches forward fondling both Gordons breasts pinching them tensely leaving ligature marks on his bare skin. Gordon screaming for him to stop Stephen swings his hand around his mouth clamping it shut. Nicholas then wiggles his flailing breasts as they ridicule a helpless Gordon. Next Nicholas raises his open palm and slaps Gordons unclad tummy just above his belly button vigorously. Repeating a second time, then a third slap discharging glaring crimson hand prints on Gordons pale skin.

NICHOLAS (CONT'D)

God can't help you Gordy when your pregnant with the devil's son. Boy you have an eating problem that we got to fix.

From inside the school Mrs. Frank hears the commotion and cachinnations from the posse lampooning Gordon from the corner of the yard.

MRS. FRANK

Quit hitting that boy you pests.

Hearing Mrs. Frank yelling from across the yard Nicholas stops and he and his chums drop Gordons arms and run across the street away from the school. Fleeing the scene taking a fast look back at Gordon as he tries to regain his power and stand up. Making eye contact with Gordon for a trice then turning and sprinting behind his buddies to avoid discipline from Mrs. Frank.

MRS. FRANK (CONT'D)

Are you alright Gordon.

Mrs. Frank walking over towards Gordon across the yard to help.

GORDON

I'm fine. I'm going home.

As Gordon stands fixing his shirt for a second then reaching down to the ground to pick up the apple with the pencil still stuck in it. Holding it up and brushing off the dirt then pulling out the pencil he walks away the opposite direction from Nicholas and everyone else. Visibly skittish and cuckoo baring a self hating grin he breaks the pencil in half and drops the broken pieces to the ground walking away alone sobbing quietly. Thinking to himself he pictures Nicholas face in his mind. Then imagines gazing at Nicholas's crotch as he stands up in front of him bitterly remembering what just happened to him he fantasizes stabbing Nicholas in the groin with the pencil. Envisioning blood streaming down Nicholas's legs he shows a simper as he continues meandering home alone along the stone paved road towards his house.

LOOKING DIRECTLY DOWN AT THE STONE ROAD AS GORDONS CHUBBY FEET STEP AHEAD -------------------
--WALKING HOME

FADE OUT.

DRUNK BOY TRICKED

INSIDE A CROWDED SALOON IN DOWNTOWN NEW HAVEN CONNECTICUT

Dapper 23 year old Christoper with alluring blond locks and a lissome build finishes his last sip from his draft sitting at the bar in a crowded downtown saloon. Rambunctious men and flirtatious women beleaguering him and being clamorous. He slams the empty glass on the bar in front of him and asks the bartender for another.

CHRISTOPHER

I've got myself a fine date to attend in twenty minutes I must fancy myself a worthy drunk first.

BARTENDER

Have a blackstrap this shall help you with your mood. Good luck with the dame.

The bartender pours him a blackstrap as an elder man also in good shape like Christopher sporting a full black beard and mustache sits down next to him distinctly boozed.

DRUNK GUY

Who are you? Why is the only seat left in this place next to a damn boy. There's a good number of women here and stacks of pretty ones but they all came escorted by at least three hairy assholes I swear.

CHRISTOPHER

I already got me the hottest date tonight all set up. Cheryl is expecting me at her place after I finish this here blackstrap. She is mighty sexy and showed me around this saloon earlier, first time for me tonight.

Christopher raises his glass up to the drunk guy and then takes a lasting shwig emptying it half way then setting it in front of him on the bar.

DRUNK GUY

Why isn't this Cheryl here with you now, boy.

CHRISTOPHER

Her rich daddy asked her to meet some friends of his down the street a short bit ago but I got her house number and she wants me to tryst with her there soon. No need looking any further I got me what I came here for, it can't get any better tonight for me.

DRUNK GUY

How do you know this lady isn't playing with you boy. I've seen me a fair number of fake gals in this city.

CHRISTOPHER

Fake gals. Never heard.

DRUNK GUY

Yes I don't shit you this. The fudge ladies who just pretend to tease boys like you do exist, ladies with dicks.

BARTENDER

He's telling you the truth I've seen the kind here myself.

As he pours a blackstrap for the drunk guy.

CHRISTOPHER

Well a lady with a dick certainly isn't my perversion. Why do they shroud such a gross gag.

DRUNK GUY

They dig it the homosexual way. You know there's ways to find out their trick before it's too late. You must touch their real tits and feel for their nuts. These fake dodos they cushion their chests and play shy. The most evil bluff they try is they tell you their vagina is sore and they ask you to fuck them in the ass instead.

BARTENDER

No lying you see old man Red at the end of the bar. A few years back he was cheated by one of these twisted wenches and caught ill after anus sex with a bimbo. He found out too late but when he did this trick she was known as Cute Kelly before she was discovered. Cute Kelly was hung dead for his con and sickness.

CHRISTOPHER

That's damn strange never experienced a phony like that. I know a real pussy when its staring me in the face any day.

DRUNK GUY

Thought I'd give you warning you never know what's out there these days, everybody's got a hoax to play and their ruse is always routine.

CHRISTOPHER

So you say, will you tell me what your trick is then old man.

DRUNK GUY

I've got too many tricks son. My best trick is not giving them away for free at least. You got something to bargain with and I'll tell you anything you want to know.

Lifting his glass to quaff and hurling it to the bar satisfied with his blackstrap he licks his lips giving leer to the drunk guy next to him.

CHRISTOPHER

I don't have time to barter with you old man. I am gonna go get me laid, I know Cheryl is not one of theses chicks with a dick and balls. I'm gonna be touching her breasts and lick on those raging nipples then do her tight twat the way a spicy dame digs it.

Christopher stands up.

BARTENDER

You go be safe now.

DRUNK GUY

Don't come crying to me if this mare bites off your pecker when you find out she's packing a boner. It's a common affliction in blind dates like yours son. Unless your applesauce likes the meat stick, its your game to turkey.

CHRISTOPHER

Your so full of malarkey, I can take care of myself old man. I ain't a blind numskull Cheryls a ornate lady and she's gonna be my missuss after tonight I tell you. Now get your drunk on without me I have to make my way there it's a decent hoof.

As Christopher sallies away from the drunk guy and the bartender, past patrons carousing in the huddled saloon and out onto the street. Pulling a small piece of paper out of his right pocket and staring at it closely following the directions sketched and memorizing the house number, putting it back in his pocket. Christopher jaunts past numerous drunkards near the entrance and vagabonds in the street. Sauntering to his right three blocks as the darkness succumbs around him and all people disappear. Walking alone down Sugar Maple St. he continues beyond a multitude of stone houses and approaching what seems a desolate field ahead. Looking over the tall swaying grass in the wind to see if he can spot Cheryl's house. The excitement to see Cheryl transcends into a vibe of uncertainty, thinking he may have made a wrong turn he pauses but then continues forward in the still of the opaque night. Suddenly from behind him he hears a horse carriage advancing. Turning to see who is passing him he watches as a single horse pulling a covered buggy behind jogs up to where he is standing. Stopping as it reaches Christopher a mans voice from inside the covered buggy resonates through the dark conspicuously. Abe and Cy both in their early thirties and with slightly chubby builds are sitting next to each other in the buggy. Abe who is clean shaven holds the ropes guiding the horse as Cy with a bushy brown beard and mustache stares anxiously at Christopher as Abe speaks out.

ABE

Hey there boy are you lost.

CHRISTOPHER

I don't know. I am seeking 2100 block of High St. I believe I am headed the right way.

CY

High st.is a long walk ahead if you like we can give you lift. We'll take you right there.

Christopher notices a yank at the pit of his stomach recognizing the sensation as a fear of strangers especially in the gloom of the night. He fights off his jitters for a chance to arrive sooner then later he decides to accept the offer.

CHRISTOPHER

Well sure I figure I'll be happier reaching my missus quicker then my cold feet could do. Thank you sirs.

ABE

No problem at all, the air is rather chilled tonight, I am Abe and my sorry friend is Cy what's your name?

CHRISTOPHER

I'm Christopher how do you fellows do?

ABE

Were fixing to be better here shortly, Cy why don't you grab the blanket for us. You can sit in the middle its warmer between us, less wind in your face.

Abe stands and gets out of the buggy for a brief moment for Christopher to jump up on the carriage seat as Cy reaches in back retrieving a charcoal wool blanket. Christopher sitting in the middle with a look of appreciation on his face watches as Abe jumps back in and motions for the horse to take off ahead leading them past the vacant tillage.

CHRISOPHER

So you Sirs coming from town?

Pausing before answering as the horse continues forward.

ABE

You don't want to know what town we are from and to be frank your never going to find out.

As he and Cy reach for their guns hidden next to their hips they simultaneously point their revolvers up against Christophers temples on each side of his head. Groped with shock he sits still not wanting to be shot.

CHRISTOPHER

What do you want from me. I don't have much with me I am on my way to get laid I spent my ration on my rum back in town I swear.

CY

Do we look as dumb as your mother. Shut your mouth before we blow your foggy brains onto that horses ass.

Abe and Cy clenching their revolvers tight against each side of Christophers head while he is encompassed with terror beyond any he has felt before. Remaining unconditionally inert and silent he figures there is no way out from his captors.

ABE

You do have a pretty little mouth now don't you.

As Abe reaches the gun towards Christophers lips he maneuvers the barrel slowly into his mouth.

CHRISTOPHER

Please Sir I don't want to die.

CY

Who said you are going to die. At least not yet stop being a sissy and suck on Abes gun like it was your own hard prick.

ABE

You practice on my piece, show us what your pretty mouth can do because if you want to live that wet hole of yours is going to have to do its job on me.

CY

And when your done with your gig on us both we will decide if we are satisfied. Maybe we'll let you live for more, maybe not.

ABE

If you piss me off and stop doing your chore with that wet hole wide open son, it's going to be the last taste of beef you ever have before hell.

CY

If you use those damned teeth and bite me your going to die slow and painful because we'll tear your own damned prick off and leave you tied up to bleed yourself a despicable death for a beggar.

Abe slowly pulls the barrel of his gun out from Christophers mouth and with his other hand begins to undo his pants. Signaling the horse to a complete stop on the side of the dirt road there is nothing but open countryside on each side of the carriage.

CHRISTOPHER

I'll do anything you want just don't kill me please.

ABE

Ain't it this bastards lucky day he stumbled his ass the wrong way out of town. High st. is back the other direction boy your mistake now it's time for me and Cy to get us laid.

Reaching his other hand around the top of Christophers golden blond hair and directing his head lower.

CY

How's come you always get your way with em first, I told you our luck would be better down this road. It should be my turn getting my way first.

ABE

Shut your pie hole Cy I can't get off with your whiny voice yelling mad at me. You'll have your turn next now fuck off.

Christopher complying to their demands. Cy discreetly masturbating to the other side of Christopher grabs a hold of his hair shortly after Abe sighs in delectation and pushes his head onto himself.

ABE (CONT'D)

Now keep quiet and enjoy while we still own this asshole.

Obeying Cy's imposition the same as Abe Christopher caving in in faithful manner in order to survive the nighttide. Abe fixing his pants as Cy has his way with Christopher in quietude. After the sodomy Cy lifts Christopher up by his hair and swings the butt of his revolver callously knocking him unconscious swiftly. Abe whacking him a second time to assure he is entirely blacked out, then picks up his motionless body shoving it behind them in the buggy. Cy covering Christopher with the blanket as Abe commands the horse to turn around abruptly.

THE HORSE LEADING THE CARRIAGE BACK INTO TOWN DOWN THE DIRT COUNTRY ROAD
DISSOLVE TO:
THE NIGHT SKY FILLED WITH STARS
FADE TO:
JAILED FOR BUGGERY
THE JAIL FLOOR AS CHRISTOPHER LAYS SPRAWLED OUT ASLEEP

Opening his eyes slowly for the first time since the night before Christopher awakens to the stinging of pain from the top of his head as he reaches his right hand to console his injury. Trying hard not to sob he clasps his other hand in anger and lifts his head to look around the damp and lurid jail floor. The only other person in the small 8 by 10 cell is Roger an ashen haired man with average build and matching shaggy beard sitting with his back against the cell wall and two feet spread out in front of him.

ROGER
It's just you and me in this god forsaken place.

CHRISTOPHER
What happened to me, why am I here. Where am I?

ROGER
Don't you know your own story kid. They dropped you in here with me a few hours ago. This cell is solely for the drunk shysters to sober up. They'll keep you in this nasty dung hole for days with a few sparse bread crumbs and just let you vomit your way to sobriety or they keep you here to dawdle.

CHRISTOPHER
What did they freakin' toss me here for I never did nobody no harm.

ROGER
From what I heard that blockhead jailor saying you been accused of buggery kid. Two folk turned you in last night said you tried bargaining homosexual boon with them for a ride to your womans place. At least that's what I heard myself I could be wrong my stinking ears have all but sold out on me over the years.

CHRISTOPHER
That ain't the truth I've been robbed and trampled last night. I can't believe I'm still alive those lying thieves are going to pay for what they did.

ROGER
You got some time to pay here for buggery kid first.

CHRISTOPHER
Buggery, my ass. Those crooks were bullshitting thinking they can just have their way with me like this. I didn't do nothing to piss off God why is my fate so cruel to me. I'm going to find those filthy heisters, I'm nobodys patsy one day they'll get their sortie I promise you.

As Christopher gathers himself and pushes himself into a sitting position with his back up against the cell wall like Rogers. Sitting a few feet apart Christopher looks over at Roger soothing his head wounds.

ROGER
You know your family is going to have to treat you like a queer now you been caught and arrested.

CHRISTOPHER

My family doesn't have to find out about this I'll tell them I found myself a job out of town for a bit. I don't know why everyone hates homosexuals so much anyhow I never had one do anything wrong to me before this.

ROGER

Before last night you suppose. Those folk accusing you were saying they were from New York and just passing through if that helps any. Whatever happened to you is your own kooky business anyway.

A hole in the wall is opened by the jailor on the other side.

JAILOR

You two fools can just share your only meal tonight. I'll see you jokers at first light to take you to the magistrate.

Dropping a small plate with bread crumbs and few displaced green peas for the prisoners. Two runty cups filled with sooty water are placed on the plate with the tiny portion of leftovers. Then the hole is closed as Roger crawls over picking up the plate and carrying it over towards Christopher. Setting it on the floor between them as he moves closer to him and picks up a bread crumb to snack on. Christopher plucks bread crumbs and stuffs his mouth as the two prisoners sit flippantly clearing the plate. Roger fingering the last green pea and holding in front of his face before flinging it at Christophers face playfully.

CLOSE UP OF THE GREEN PEA IN AIR AND THEN BOUNCING OFF CHRISTOPHERS CHEEK TO THE FLOOR.

Roger chuckles then picks up the rolling pea off the floor and eats it. Christopher laughing back at Roger finding him humorous as they rest their backs against the wall smiling aspiring to bypass sheer boredom. A few middling moments of silence pass as Christopher stares at the sullied walls confining him.

CHRISTOPHER

So who lied for you to be here, are you being accused of buggery too.

ROGER

No, I was just very washed down the other night at a tavern in town. To tell you the truth I can't remember what happened or what I did. When I woke up in here they told me I had another 2 days to sober up before they tell me why I'm here.

CHRISTOPHER

You are one over boozed old man aren't you.

Roger acting mad at Christophers comment lunges towards him again playfully but squeezing his arms with both hands lightly. Christopher recognizing his softness doesn't react and allows him to squeeze his arms.

ROGER

I may be spent and dopey for an old man and for getting myself tossed in here with you kid but at least I'm not a dead old man. If I didn't enjoy a fresh young kid like you here helping me pass my time I'd let you have it.

CHRISTOPHER

Well you show me a good way to pass the time, old man. I'm all out of ideas myself.

Without hesitation Roger lowers his face towards Christophers groin and with both his hands gropes his crotch undoing his pants hurriedly and without word. Revering the reticence Christopher decides not to intervene avowing Roger to rapidly get him erect and perform oral. Leaning his head back on the cell wall mollifyingly and with flair sweet on Roger's performance he shuts his eyes. A minute blows past in quiescence as the Roger progresses an elongated session of fixation. As this is occurring the jailor fortuitously opens the cell doors and catches squint of Roger and Christopher together on the floor. Separating as soon as they see the door opening but too late not to be seen by the jailor Roger backs away from Christopher. Leaning up against the cell wall across from him as Christopher scrambles swiftly to button his pants assuring he is no longer exposed in front of the raving Jailor.

JAILOR

Boy you and your pappy are going to hang for this. Unnatural offences call for death at the gallows. The Jailor slams shut the door.

CLOSE UP OF CHRISTOPHER FINISHING PULLING UP HIS TROUSERS

FADE TO BLACK.

A HAND AND A HANGING FOR SODOMY

The limpid morning light shines down on a crush of spectators surrounding the gallows and the bludgeoning noose hanging before the rabble.

LOOKING THROUGH THE NOOSES LOOP AT ROGER AS HE IS BEING USHERED PAST THE MOB TOWARDS THE GALLOWS.

Arriving at his final destination Roger is pegged into the noose and hanged before the cheering commonality. Scoffing and burlesque echo as he hangs gravely granting death to poach his flogged body. FROM BELOW ROGERS TWO FEET AS THEY SUCCUMB TO A STOP LOOKING UP AT HIS BODY AS IT DIES IN THE GRASP OF THE NOOSE AROUND HIS NECK

Christopher is escorted onto the platform next to Roger as he remains drooping stiff. His arms are being held by courtsmen as a table is set in front of him by the heralds. Thwacking Christophers right arm oblate on the table in vista of the riffraff as they observe scrupulously in travesty.

COURTSMAN

Today the court is going to teach this callow sodomite right and wrong. He was caught in the act of an unnatural crime with another man this morning. Normally this means instant death like his consort homosexual sinner who has just suffered euthanasia for us all here today. We have concluded god has a liberal plan for this plagued transgressors life. After we cut off his best hand and banish him from our state forever. We shall alibi fate to absolve this convicted sodomites fortune and death shall seal it if he steps foot in our state ever again.

      (Pause)

Let him have it.

A courtsman swinging a thick axe blade cuts off Christophers entire right hand as bloods scuds across his mutated arm and the table.

SLOW MOTION OF CHRISTOPHERS HAND AS IT FALLS FROM THE TABLE INTO A BASKET BELOW.

Christophers bare chest now spattered with fresh blood as his cleaved arm dangles in paroxysm while the throng cheers in raillery. Convoyed towards a carriage to be led off and dropped for ultimate deportation.

FADE OUT.

BONFIRE BONING

A LARGE BONFIRE BURNING AND SMOKING CROSSING THE FLAMES

Tobias's face admiring the night tide still on his extremity while Sebastian appears aloft his crux gaping into his eyes. Thrusting himself profoundly and raptly beaming at each other savoring the moment. Sebastian pauses in gloat above Tobias's face in sheer proximity.

SEBASTIAN

You don't like girls much do you Toby.

Resting beside Tobias's side grazing his right arm with his left, the bonfire aglow a few feet away.

TOBIAS

I never said that, I like the ones who don't act like they know everything at least.

SEBASTIAN

What about me, Toby. Do I know everything. Everything you want me to know at least.

TOBIAS

Ill never let anybody know your secret if that's what you mean.

SEBASTIAN

Best friends forever, promise.

TOBIAS

Promise

SEBASTIAN

Its time for you to come work with me Toby. I want you to do what I do up at the pub. You'll never need to drudge, it's the best calling a man can accept.

TOBIAS

A job?

SEBASTIAN

Yes it's a perfect proposition. All the brothers there will give you well Toby. They give me well especially when I minister them what they crave.

TOBIAS

What do you pose them?

SEBASTIAN

It depends on the guy Toby but just what they want, whatever I'm comfortable with. Me and the boys tend the bar at nights. Its a worthy keep and I want you to start with me tomorrow night, Ill show you everything you need to know.

TOBIAS

Sounds like you do yourselves a lot of boozing. Last time we binged you taught me to wrestle. Your going to have to train me to hold my guts in if I drink too much.

SEBASTIAN

I'll make sure your heads up while your sipping and tending the bar with me. I'll make you proud to be a pub boy. You'll be treated and taken care of every night. All you got to do is learn what you like and it'll like you back.

TOBIAS

What if people there think I like you too much.

SEBASTIAN

You'll cotton to all the boys who slosh Toby. I'm sure after a few nights you'll know everybody up there better. That's the good part and why all the boarders come back.

TOBIAS

I'll just tell my pop you found me a job working nights after school and everything.

SEBASTIAN

Your pop will be glad just tell him your helping out up at the pub with things. Bring him home some rum and punch the first night.

TOBIAS

Yea. Pop would love himself some rum and punch.

SEBASTIAN

You'll love the pub Toby.

Teasing Tobias rubbing his sleek abdomen briefly then rolling on top of him. His legs encompassing his mid section focusing on Tobias's simper.

FADE OUT.

TRICK OF THE TRADE

Inside a smoke filled parlour room of an ample north end Boston manor.

SCOTT

This villa is our turf all the kosher boys here get exactly what they dig.

SAMUEL

Many cranks will do whatever is wanted for pumped up kicks usually barter coins and boon.

ROBERT

Our house is a gratis market, our customers are bona fide and usually returns.

Zac and Jacob slurping flips at a table with Josh and Terry, twin 21 year old tawnies.

JOSH

They don't call us the pixie twins for nothing. Look what this ogre red bearded man dickered us last night, just for 5 minutes with both of us.

Plopping a solid gold belt buckle and matching gold clock chain onto the round log table. Zac spanking fists with Josh as they burst.

JOSH (CONT'D)

You should of seen it when he finished with us that pudgy red beard hopped up and did a dance like this. Josh raising his hands above his head twisting both wrists and spinning in two circles fast reenacting the dance cracking.

TERRY

I've topped that, check what this brute dealt me last week. He told me to use it if any bastard forces me do something I don't agree to.

Terry reaching up under a loose section of floorboard and flaunting a burnished black pistol. Gripping both hands and pointing at Jacob scoffing as if to shoot then brandishing it towards the ceiling.

JACOB

How long have you been playing these ponies?

TERRY

We've been in this hood since we were 15. The pixie twins own Boston.

Terry and Josh smack each others chests.

FADE OUT.

A ROOM WITH A RUSE

THE SHIPYARD IN MANHATTAN AT MID DAY SUN SHINING AND CROWDED WITH SHIPBUILDERS

Seymour freelancing with his cutlass on surplus logs waiting for the crew to come to cahoots. Discerning Morgans glamour following his movements from the adjacent side of the shipyard with his eyes. Thrilled by the prestige of his newfound mate hungrily anticipating days spire to liaison.

MORGAN AND SEYMOUR CONVERGE WALKING TOGETHER AS THEY LEAVE THE SHIPYARD AT DAYS END.

Arriving outside the White Rose Tavern which is walking distance of the shipyard. Seymour entering first with Morgan contiguous behind him, and greets Garret. Standing taller then the rest at 6'3 and with curly longish cocoa frizzies, tender blue eyes and hardy figure he and Seymour hug cordially.

GARRET

Whos your buddy never seen him in here before?

SEYMOUR

This is Morgan's first time at the Rose. He's getting the grand tour of the facilities today and I want him to meet everybody.

Morgan and Garret shake hands sweetly and mirror inquiring ganders.

GARRET

Welcome to the Rose Morgan here the partying and brews don't stop.

SEYMOUR

Some of the other guys from the yard love their coolers here I bet we will run into a number of them later.

Brad wearing his sleeves rolled up carrying two cannikins and with the top button of his trousers undone but ostensibly not detecting. He avenues Seymour and Morgan dishing out both of them an imbued cannikin of beer.

BRAD

So is this the kid with the skills you were bragging about who wants a good job.

SEYMOUR

Yes. This is Morgan I'm going to show him around some and let him get drunk and acquainted for the first time.

BRAD

Its a rule in our house if you stay with us you must love to slosh. Love all the guys you share the house with. Homage is a virtue at the Rose, there are no strangers here.

MORGAN

I can handle that.

GARRET

Another rule of the pub is if your serving in our house you need to keep fit. We don't esteem jelly belly or dingy slackers providing our hootch. We got a reputation to keep, top notch always.

MORGAN

I got ya. Im sure you have lots of rich folks coming in.

SEYMOUR

The Rose is known for its endowment with our cortege. We don't disappoint and it never gets boring. There's always 3 or 4 us moonlighting every night we got to keep up with the demands and our customers deed us well.

Sitting at a table in the back Todd, Paul, Stephen and Timmy are playing cards and tossing beers.

TODD

Garret hook us up some rotgot will ya.

Seymour leads Morgan past a few empty tables in the center of the tavern towards the back table where his friends are.

SEYMOUR

Weekends in this place we are choked wall to wall all night. Guys wait in the back and along the sides for a spot at the tables. We just added four new rooms in back because the Rose is popular with the boys who splurge. We need to have enough space for them to spree and relieve themselves in peace. Plus everyones always blown and if you piss on our floor your done for the night. I'll show you our brand new wash rooms and privies next.

As Seymour walks up to the table spanking hands with Todd as he sits in front of his cards and beer mug.

TODD

So who's the new kid?

SEYMOUR

Im showing Morgan our pub today let him decide for himself if he wants an extra job sucking them down with us mature boys in the evenings.

MORGAN

Sucking down suds is a pretty easy job.

As Todd reaches his mug towards Morgan for a toast, then both guzzling their beer in a dead heat, Todd belches theatrically.

TODD

Cheers to drunkenness, healthy whores and modern wealth.

PAUL

Todds saving to build a ship lusty enough to take his gullible ass to the other side of the world. Todds never been to England he thinks if he visits one day he is going to inherit his loaded granpas fortunes when he passes.

STEPHEN

Everyone knows the colonies cream England. Toiling in our colonies has luxuries at least our harlots don't have diseases. Slaving to some imbecile king is rueful, and now in Boston they're killing our people in the streets.

TODD

My grandpa asked me and for all of us to work his tavern for him in Manchester, at least for a while. Its a nice place not far from the coast. More cuaint then the Rose but we could make it our summer home one day.

PAUL

Todds still dreaming about saving up for the voyage. Those cheating bastards with their damned taxes on our goods. We aren't going to give up our profits for their greed. Double-crossing us to get rich off our beer and rum. Our red-eye is all ours to score from. Dirty Georgie is going to suffer for his bamboozle, taxing our colonies. We own this land not some festering moron king across the sea.

TIMMY

Todd your Grandpa won't even consent to sail us boys over to tend his tavern with you, unless one of us wigs long quills and pretend boobs acting as your wife. He'll accuse you of being a homosexual deviant and disown you even if he doesn't catch you with his own eyes.

TODD

My grandpa was a bachelor once I'll just tell him some lie about my wife catching ill in the colonies and dying. I'll tell him a good story how I'm gonna find me a new wife soon. If not while tending his place than when I come home. Even if he accuses me of such an atrocity I'll still draw my portion of his fortune when he passes I don't see why not. I figure if I bring all you guys as bar hands to run his tavern he will cut me much more when he's gone then what I'd get if we don't help him one summer. He's so old and bald headed all his time is going to be up sooner then later I am sure of it.

SEYMOUR

Sail east to prove to him you care and make your stakes. Morgan and I can help build ya that ship you want. We'll all cipher a plan one day.

He chortles and knocks mugs with Morgan as they take a sip then thwacks mugs with Todd, Timmy, Stephen, and Paul. As Taylor an older friend of theirs in his early thirties walks up to the table.

TAYLOR

Listen up I have yall's favorite song in my head yall gotta hear me play and sing with me.

He marches over to the wall near the table where everyone is gathered and sits at the piano seat. Reciting a parody chorus of Yankee Doodle while Todd, Timmy, Stephen, and Paul stand up and surround Taylor in front of the piano. He starts buoyantly with the lyrics in articulate rendition of the popular anthem while everyone parrots in harmony. Turning to face each other as they sing in caricature. Seymour approaches Morgan closely.

SEYMOUR

Let me take you to our safe rooms.

He turns towards the far back hallway of the tavern which furnishes a red and white rug on the floor all the way to the back wall. Multiple doors remain shut on each side of the hallway with chichi brass knobs on each door and well painted exteriors. Framed paintings are hung between each door.

MORGAN

Its really nice back here.

SEYMOUR

For our orthodox bedfellows and those yet to fathom our covertness, The ones yet to discern the merriment we make sure to keep a very respectable place to appease yourself.

MORGAN

So these doors are to the washrooms.

SEYMOUR

In our house our privies dual as changing rooms and are always kept peerless and smelling admirable. We keep this top priority here and the flowing sewers were dug deep under the floor and lead far away from here. We give our health reverence at the Rose Morgan.

Leading Morgan to the last door on the right side of the hallway opening it and walking in promptly grasping Seymours linen shirt pulling him in with him and shutting the door behind him.

MORGAN

Requisite space to appease ones self, I see.

Seymour tugs Morgan's body up onto his and kisses him. Surprising Morgan at first as he welcomes the comforting endearment while Seymour caresses Morgan loosening his chemise. Slowly releasing his lips and staring into Morgan's eyes.

SEYMOUR

Privacy matters.

MORGAN

It's private here what's a matter.

SEYMOUR

This is one of our many wash rooms yes, there is more to matriculate in here, Morgan.

MORGAN

I'm listening what more is there to size up about a privy I don't have to pee, do you?

Smiling as he continues gazing into Morgan's eyes Seymour then turns his head to face the corner of the wall.

SEYMOUR

Do you see these gorgeous borders we have in our corners.

MORGAN

Yes

SEYMOUR

They are the key to this rooms trick. Only the slick boys know how to turn the trick. Your smart Morgan want to get smarter.

MORGAN

What's the trick?

SEYMOUR

Watch me and commemorate. Common recipients do not know of these rooms Morgan only the boys who cliche the game.

As he presses the inner portion of the corner border with one hand then gently pushing the wall with his other hand as it nonchalantly opens.

MORGAN

You must be smart to know how to open that door.

Seymour leads Morgan into a hidden room where a pallet covered with a thick fluffy fur highlights the interior. A lamp rests on a small table up against the far wall from the entrance. Shutting the esoteric wall door then reaching over to the table to light the lamp.

SEYMOUR

Everything that ever happens in this rein remains clandestine forever. Preserving reputation proceeds any damn allegations. Selling our secrets at the Rose is a fatal sin and those who break our first rule shall suffer the consequences with eternal banishment and even death. We have too many affluent habitue here at the Rose who repute the axiom of our hostelry and serve any and all traitors who wish to see us burn for their ill words. All heresay and lies concerning our keystone any respectable bigwig wouldn't trust anyway. Truth has it many of our evanescent frequenters are known to run this city.

Morgan sits on the sassy fur covered bed and then lays back.

MORGAN

I desire it in here.

SEYMOUR

Your shall savor and favor in here recurrently if you start helping us here at the Rose in the evenings.
Before you decide there's more perks for you to soak up but that comes tomorrow at my house. I would
like you over for a succulent dinner and exclusive parley if you oblige.

MORGAN

I shall accept the invite but I must say I don't elect waiting to surmise this game of yours out.

SEYMOUR

The aphorisms here at the Rose our partakers penchant are believed to bless us with the extramundane.

MORGAN

Then I suppose I will wait longer for you to enlighten me tomorrow if that's how you wish it.

SEYMOUR

Let me extol you the light that shines in this room.

Seymour positions his legs over top Morgan's as he relaxes with his back on the bed looking up
devotedly. Seymour extracting his own chemise off dearly, one arm at a time and tossing it gently on the
floor. Undoing Morgans for him next flinging it beside his. Morgan fondles Seymours stomach with his
hands moving them towards his chest and then back towards his navel. Disengaging his trousers first
and sliding them entirely off then doing the same to Seymours he leans forward kissing his chin and
lowering down his neck to his upper chest, concluding with his right nipple. Licking Morgan
synchronously as they become intertwined with each others bodies chaffing bare skin in concert.
Seymour turns sideways and they position themselves apropos for a 69. Itching one another cuddling
adoring both firmly matrixed anatomies.

SEYMOUR (CONT'D)

May this room caprice your fancy, Morgan in here is where we gloat but we do all float our own boat.
Ennoble your own penetralia. Are you prepared to tipple with us all tonight?

MORGAN

Lets get drunk.

SEYMOUR

Follow me, you see we can exit into the next washroom here. A knack two can ploy to covet.

Seymour chuckles as he pushes the corner border of the wall adjacent from where they came in as the
cryptic entrance leading to the neighboring wash room and privy cracks open inward. He pulls it towards
him and steps out closing the door behind Morgan. Morgan sensing a recondite curiosity sweeping his
thoughts about Seymour and the Rose as they walk down the hall together back into the main parlor
room. A well kept young man in his early twenties with curtate sepia locks and bright green eyes passes
them into the hallway sharing a polite look at one another without speaking. The parlor room has filled
with two more full tables of callers sipping in shenanigan.

CLOSE UP OF A CALLER LAYING A WINNING HAND ONTO THE TABLE FOR EVERYONE TO SEE.

CARD PLAYER

Suckers.

FADE TO BLACK.

STALKING AND BINGING FOR VENGEANCE

As the intense morning sun rises over Gordons Providence neighborhood. Gordon's kindred corpulent
mother donning rangy russet tufts below her shoulders walks into Gordons room as he lays sleeping on

his bed alone.

GORDON'S MOM

Gordon will you get your lazy butt out of bed and go to school. Your momma needs to clean house this morning.

GORDON

I'm not going today momma my stomach feels too lousy.

Gordons mom looks at Gordon with a disgusting grin and then leaves his room. Gordon shirtless and still laying in bed pulls his cover off his chest but continuing to rest on his back with the blanket covering him from the waist below. He gazes up at the ceiling in his room and then adjusts his site on his father as he rushes through the doorway all the way up to him remaining petrified. Excessively pudgy like Gordon and his mother Gordon's father raises his fist high in the air at his son.

GORDONS FATHER

You better get that big head of yours out of bed son and make your way to school right now. You talk back to your mother anymore and you'll be eating morsels off the street Gordon. We won't raise a corrupted son with such a shoddy attitude like yours Gordy. Now you listen to me get dressed and take off to school or you won't even be lucky enough to have scraps in our home for a week.

Bitterly Gordon stands and reaches for his school pants as his father rubbernecks with his fist raised. Lowering his fist as Gordon pulls up his bottoms and stretches for a pallid linen shirt near by and tussles to squash it over his blubbery frame. Taking a moment to glance over at his parents giving him a subjective leer. Gordon curtains his shirt and brushes against his moms arm subtly walking past his parents out the door leaving his home. Ambulating down the stone paved road casing his neighbors bantam homes built in tight nigh to one another. Suddenly from behind him and to his left a mutter is hearkened.

STEPHEN

Gordy your such a whale, even if your family could afford your lard ass a horse to ride you to class, you'd break both it's damn legs and spine the second you sat those dragging fat cheeks on it.

As he walks ahead of a slow paced Gordon who sneaks a peak over at Stephen speeding up even faster past him.

GORDON

What you so afraid of you shmuck you must stare at all the boys asses in class I see you noticing my cheeks for me.

STEPHEN

Pucker off you flabby faggot.

Offended from the constant insults Gordon chooses to flake off into the deep woods slumbering at the base of the tallest spruce tree he could find instead of going to school. Waking with nothing but vengeance on his mind he surmises a plan for reprisal before returning home due to hunger pains.

FADE OUT.

BURNING BLOOD OF A BLACKSMITH

THE HOT ORANGE BURNING BUTT OF A CHAIR LEG BEING MELT INTO SHAPE

Gerard 26 year old son of a renowned blacksmith with curtailed black tufts and copper brown eyes. Standing 6 foot 2 and a lean 150 pounds of experienced sleekness and muscle. Taught everything there is to master from the trade of a blacksmith by his acclaimed father who has owned a shop in downtown Raleigh, North Carolina for 20 years. Molding chairs, bells, fireplaces and muskets for his customers 47 year old Denny Shaver has built the reputation as the best Blacksmith in the Carolinas and imbued his son everything he knows to aid him in operation of his blacksmith business. Gerard the only son of a family of five who all live in the same house above the shop in Raleigh. Freelancing vaingloriously in the dimly lit cellar workspace Gerard continues with the sculpting of a chair leg as his father opens the door and down the few stone steps into the workspace.

DENNY

How's the leg coming along son?

GERARD

Almost done pop, just give me a few more seconds.

As he ceases the last touches on the leg and pulls the scorching red edge off the table and panoramas it for his father to view.

DENNY

Glad to see you know what your doing son and doing it the right way. I tell you what Gerard we have lots of business coming our way to execute. Since David left for Virginia the other day I must hire two solid hands to support us full time.

GERARD

Do you know which of the prents you are going to ask to do the job.

DENNY

Well I thought I would I let you answer that question. I know you've been tutoring Bobby, Dawson, Billy and Timmy for the last month. Why don't you choose the two most talented hands and give them word we want them here helping us a full day from now on. Tell them we shall pay them proper blacksmith wage and if they do quality work we intend to double it in 3 months time.

GERARD

Sure thing how about I see each of the prents for one last lesson tomorrow. They are scheduled from morning through the afternoon I see all of them separately and will break the news to the two I decide possess the deserving knack to be with us full time.

DENNY

Great Gerard, thanks I will wait for your final decision at dinner tomorrow. How about you take the rest of the day off I will stay and wrap up with these silver bells, go have some fun with your friends son.

GERARD

Thanks pop. Tomorrow will be a good time picking the two crackerjacks.

DENNY

If you do your job well and both neophytes deliver for us I will boost your wage too Gerard.

Gerard walks towards the egress as Denny lifts the calcine chair leg perusing his son's work on the blazing metal.

GERARD

I'll deliver for you pop I promise.

Loping up the steps and outside onto the downtown Raleigh street as a clique of teens revel across the street spinning tops and wisecracking. Gerard foots by the group smirking but not saying anything continuing past them. A rebellious boy picks up the top as it spins on the cobblestone then hurls it hard at the back of Gerards head. The top bounces off his skull as it rolls to a stop. All the teens burst hysterically jeering him as the boy who heaved it screeches at Gerard.

BOY

That's for laughing at us big head.

GERARD

You squirt.

As Gerard races towards the aggregation as the teens take off running away down the middle of the street.

GERARD (CONT'D)

You better keeping running or I'm going to make you all squirt in your cruddy bloomers if you throw any more of your damn toys at my head.

The teens keep sprinting and crackling.

BOY

Well come and get yourself some squirt you won't get any unless you catch us.

The boy flipping Gerard a birdie and scurrying away behind his fleeing friends. Gerard watches as the sprouts get away and giggles murmuringly to himself before turning around and promenading back towards his fathers shop.

FADE OUT.

DELAWARE COAST CATERWAULING

The burnt apricot colored sun setting over the Atlantic Coast reflecting off the ocean water all the way up to the pristine Delaware sand. Thaddeus twirling his mid ear length strawberry blond locks rests cross legged on the beach staring out at the ocean as the sun sets to the west. Snacking on an orange he drops the last peel onto the sand and bites into the juicy climactic part of his meal for the day. Startled from behind an older brazen looking man approaches him. His age pomps through his graying hair and short beard. A slight belly protuding his shirt ricochetting the awkward stranger feeling.

RICKY

Your the only one out here tonight I see. Would you like some company for a bit lad?

THADDEUS

Well I don't know how much longer I am going to stay. I am finishing my last bite now but sure I have nothing else going on.

RICKY

What's your name lad? I am Ricky.

THADDEUS

I am Thaddeus.

RICKY

I've had a good friend named Thaddeus but that was years ago. So tell me what do you like the most about this part of the beach?

THADDEUS

Just seemed a great spot to gobble my orange.

RICKY

I come to these beaches quite often. I find young guys like you out here. Everyone who comes to this part of the beach alone wants something. All the guys around here know what happens here.

THADDEUS

What happens on the beach you mean?

RICKY

You know what I mean. So you don't have a lady taking care of you back home I assume that's why you like these beaches, right.

THADDEUS

Well who wouldn't like the beach especially at this time the sky is so fine.

Ricky maneuvers closer to Thaddeus as he becomes apprehensive but doesn't move away or tell Ricky to leave. Having faith in the stranger encounter Thaddeus tries to succor himself staying calm by remaining still while Ricky dips his way.

RICKY

Just relax son it's getting dark and there is no one around I checked already its just you and I tonight. I'm only going to help you relieve some stress.

Sensing Ricky was making a move on him his stomach becoming slightly queasy and uneasy with a man twice his age touching him on his upper thigh gently and rubbing his hand up towards his crotch fastly. He wants to tell him to stop and to run away at first but keeps cool and shuts his eyes to ease the site of Ricky probing him. Afraid if he immediately denies his advance he may become violent and even kill him. With his eyes shut it is easier for him to assent a hand reaching into his pants and groping his penis. Ricky candidly hooked starts to abrade himself with his open hand at the same time. A few prying minutes elapse as Ricky becomes more aggressive stroking Thaddeus who even though he has kept his eyes shut the entire time isn't pertinent to annex full erection. Ricky keeps trying as he embarks masturbating himself laying in the soothing sand next to Thaddeus his left side slathered onto Thaddeus's right leg.

RICKY (CONT'D)

Would it help you to stay hard lad if you touched me at the same time?

Opening his eyes and looking down at his penis being held by Ricky's aged wrinkly hand and reflexing revolt he can't bare the vex and jumps up quickly as Ricky slumps over watching him intently.

THADDEUS

I can't do this sorry I just don't feel good something is wrong. I am going to head home now.

Thaddeus scampering away from Ricky dwelling exposed on his side in the sand abstains from chasing after Thaddeus and watches him leave.

RICKY

Quitters are cowards son. Will you let me finish another time Thaddeus.

THADDEUS

Maybe someday. I must go home now my stomach feels rotten I am sorry.

Thaddeus continues fleeing Ricky staying on the beach but distancing himself at an urgent pace. Ricky faintly spits into the sand and then falls back staring up the dark purple streaks in the setting sky.

CLOSE UP OF THADDEUS'S FACE WALKING ALONG THE BEACH NEAR THE WATER LINE

He lingers for another 15 minutes thinking to himself about what just happened and planning his next day the sun is almost beyond the horizon as the sky is darkening fast. Suddenly to his left 30 feet away next to some petty shrubs preceding the contour of the shore he notices what seems to be two men in their late twenties or younger. Both laying on the ground one on top of the other. Stopping for the first time since deserting Ricky Thaddeus is startled by his discovery and doesn't want to disturb the two young men. At the same time one of them sees Thaddeus as he points him out to his lover and they both look over. Recognizing they have spotted him he continues slowly plodding forward. The two men stand remaining naked and ramble in Thaddeus's direction together. Thaddeus makes eye contact for the first time alluding the expressions on the mens faces arise chummy.

NAKED MAN # 1

Boy there is no reason to be scared of us. We aren't here to pick a fight.

They approach Thaddeus who remains calm but still uncomfortable with the situation.

NAKED MAN # 2

Come on boy we want you to come swimming with us. There's no better time then the gloaming.

As he reaches around Thaddeus's shoulder accommodating to remove his pullover for him.

NAKED MAN # 1

Everyone who swims in the sea with us must swim naked.

Snatching Thaddeus's cut off britches and tugs them down to his knees while his lover bungs Thaddeus's pullover to the sand.

THADDEUS

Well if you guys insist I do like to swim.

Stepping out of his britches as the two lovers run into the water diving in head first. Thaddeus standing stripped on the beach observing them. Recovering from the splash and looking back at Thaddeus.

NAKED MAN # 2

Hurry dive in. Come play with us.

As he kisses his man and they wrap their hands around each other while Thaddeus hurtles into the ocean. His head dunking under a few feet away. Surfacing he sees them frenching before lunging towards him frisking him under the water from all angles.

NAKED MAN # 1

You have such a beautiful body.

NAKED MAN # 2

Do you like to watch and be worshipped?

THADDEUS

I'll try anything once.

Naked Man # 1 dips his head under water licking on Thaddeus's nipples as his thatch barely sticking up from the waters top. Naked Man # 2 moves from Thaddeus's side to position himself behind his lover. Naked Man # 1 tonguing on Thaddeus's chest poking his head up and kisses him while his lover gently thrusts into him from the rear. Naked Man # 2 clenching his buttocks with his hands then smearing his open hands up his back passionately. Naked Man # 1 smacking Thaddeus's lips the whole time as the amethyst sky fades into full blown dusk. The random caressing session cusps in a shake as the lovers surrender together and stammer to land.

NAKED MAN # 2

We love your body. I hope you like what you see too. We must leave now we have a long walk home tonight.

NAKED MAN # 1

We will keep an eye out for you we take the same path of beach to these parts. Be safe during moonlight sometimes there are unsavory floaters who will try to take advantage of you if your not careful. Luck shall bring us together again another night I promise, take care.

THADDEUS

I'll be vigilant I know where I am headed.

NAKED MAN # 2

Thanks for the show boy, see ya next time.

The denuded lovers scatter away to their clothes by the shrubs dressing and departing west. Marooning Thaddeus soaking wet stark naked and alone on the beach in classic darkness. Decamping Thaddeus feeling used and dirty as the drama fades with the drips off his skin. Dressing fleetly he begins jogging beside the crashing waves the stars blinking into his thoughts. Trying to clear his head a small tear begins to smear down his cheek while he trots. Stopping a few minutes later from lassitude he lapses to the sand a few feet from the skirt of the hissing ocean.

FADE TO BLACK.

SPECIAL LESSONS FOR THE CHOSEN

26 year old son of a renowned blacksmith Gerard is drudging behind a scalding butt of a stake molding it in the basement workspace alone. Suddenly the door at the crest of the steps opens and young Bobby arriving for the first apprentice lesson of the day scoots spiritedly down the stone steps towards Gerard.

GERARD

Hey Bobby your a few minutes early today I see you must like this kind of work.

BOBBY

I love it.

GERARD

Then lets get started.

Bobby sporting eyebrow length cinnamon brown hair, slender with a delicate frame stands next to Gerard handing him the safe end of the scorching 3 feet long stake. Gerard beginning the lesson with his 19 year old apprentice poised behind him coxswaining his arms practicing a technique with the molding without speaking.

GERARD (CONT'D)

Bobby tell me how much you really like doing this work.

BOBBY

A lot I think I am getting damn good at it.

Maintaining to stand abaft Bobby, Gerard descends his right hand onto the lower bite of Bobbys abdomen.

GERARD

My father asked me to find the two finest apprentices I have to commission with us full time. If you do everything I want you to do today Bobby you'll be earning as much as me in a month.

Gerard shifts his hand below groping Bobby's crotch teasing his bulge. Squirming slightly and feeling apprehensive at first but simmering down after a moment thinking about his future. Bobby remains silent and concedes to Gerard fondling him even harder. Surmising the proposition convincing himself to approve Gerard touching him under his breeches onto his bare skin propped up against his buttocks with his body.

GERARD (CONT'D)

You tell nobody of this ever and the job is yours. Starting tomorrow same time.

Jerking down Bobbys breeches to his ankles he presses his hand flat against his back pushing his torso forward and leaning his twiggy body onto the side of the work table. Squeezing his bald haunches with his palms and widening his cheeks as he undoes his own breeches dropping them. Squashing Bobbys torso further forward so his stomach braces against the top of the table. The burning rim of the iron stake is pushed onto the ground as it chars idle a few feet away making space on the work table for them both. Gerard penetrates Bobbys tender skin as his legs are spread farther open. Keeping quiet while Gerard savors the sex with his budding apprentice panting in thrill. Bobby appearing to favor the sex with Gerard does not try to stop him while it lasts.

GERARD (CONT'D)

Do you accept the job Bobby?

BOBBY

Yes.

The nooky persists while Gerard scrapes his fingers on his neck.

GERARD

Nobody knows about us you swear?

BOBBY

I swear.

Gerard orgasms then yanks up his breeches as Bobby follows with his. Gerard walks around to the other side of the table picking up the singed stake and faces Bobby.

GERARD

You made the right choice Bobby you'll be treated as sterling working for us from now on. So same time tomorrow I think you can use your artistry to your benefit and you'll be earning a supreme living as an honest blacksmith. No more apprenticeship Bobby you got the perfect moil with us now, your done for today.

BOBBY

Thanks Gerard I'll see ya tomorrow.

Faking a smile at his boss then turning retreating the same way he entered. Gerard proceeds drudging alone on the work table for the next few minutes. Abruptly the door opens again and Dawson ambles into the basement workspace and approaches Gerard.

DAWSON

Looks like you don't need any help today.

Dawson donning his brunette curls teases Gerard as he looks up from his position toiling. Dawsons plump appearance as the heaviest of the 3 other apprentices razzes in Gerards mind while he sizes Dawson up with a galled look.

GERARD

Dawson if you want to find out what an honest blacksmith does to be a well paid and respected blacksmith one day you need to want to work. I've shown you how to mend legs before. Today you can work on your own finishing up the rest of what I started. I'll come back down when your done.

As Gerard points to the 3 leg stakes waiting to be mended and jilts the basement allowing Dawson to work on his own. Meandering up the steps outside into the sunlight spotting a clique of teens tossing marbles and spinning tops on the street.

FADE OUT.

Dawson finishes up his lesson alone in the basement putting out the scolding iron into a bucket of water near by. Cleaning off his hands with a towel and choosing not to wait for Gerard to return he walks up the steps and exits onto the street. Gerard is engaged in a contest of tops with the teens laughing in a circle spinning as Dawson walks past Gerard.

DAWSON

Jobs done.

GERARD

Thanks Dawson seems you finished up rather fast today how about you take tomorrow off and I'll see you Wednesday.

DAWSON

Sure thing boss.

Dawson saunters away down the crowded street and Gerard notices Billy arriving early for his lesson. Billy is the shortest of the apprentices and keeps his dark hair buzzed as bound as possible. Uniquely emaciated Billy clowns with his teacher poking Gerard softly in his belly.

BILLY

Do we have a hard lesson today teach or do we get to stay out here and flop tops instead.

As he picks up a top and spins it while the teens gibber and hee haw.

GERARD

I tell you what Billy you beat me at a match of cribbage and you can take the day off how about that.

BILLY

I'll take you up on that offer teach.

They commence a quick match of cribbage on the cobblestone while the whippersnappers rubberneck. Dogging each other as they cavort for the next few minutes and their match culminates with Gerard bellowing in victory.

GERARD

Looks like you want to keep this job Billy. Come on kid I have a commodity to brandish you after the lesson, maybe next match you'll get lucky.

BILLY

You better know that was last time you ever beat me. I won't let you get that lucky with me anymore I guarantee it.

As Gerard leads Billy down to the cellar shutting the door behind them vamoosing the dickens to carry on in the streets. Gerard slapping Billy gently on top of his head hurrying past him down the steps and postures in front of the exorbitant work table in the midpoint of the room, facing Billy while he boogies up to his abecedary.

GERARD

Billy you try hard to be funny around me I've noticed.

BILLY

I try hard at a lot of things teach.

GERARD

I tell you what Billy if you make your teacher happy today with that funny face of yours you can have a job here with us at our shop. You will be earning as much as I make in a month. If you impress in 3 months we shall double your wage. My father told me to hire two of my admirable prents for the position and I want you.

BILLY

So I don't need to learn anything more.

GERARD

I qualify you as a very smart boy I think you've learned everything you need to know.

Evulsing Billy closer to him, standing more then 6 inches taller he scans his face grinning and buffing the sides of both Billy arms with his hands. He then reaches his right hand towards the peak of Billy's head as he loosens his own drawers with his right hand and then wraps his left hand around Billy's right. Pulling Billys hand slowly towards the bump flaring out of his drawers and wrapping Billy's hand around his erection. Seduced by Gerards attraction as a friendly gesture between teacher and apprentice he accords to Gerard's penchant while he captains his head lower hoodwinking Billy into oral sex. Gerard trickling his fingernails softly on his cheeks and forehead.

MEMORY OF BILLY AND HIS FRIEND TEASING EACH OTHER THEN MAKING OUT

Billy cottoning to the experience while he remembers similiar past occasions making out with a friend of his. Reveling in his full blown fantasy enduring through capsheaf, lifting his head up now regarding Gerard in a higher light. Arousal eating at him inside while he stands and Gerard kneels unraveling Billys fly and reciprocating. Lasting longer performing for his rook to crown before standing caulking his drawers for him and then his own.

GERARD (CONT'D)

That's good enough for us today Billy. You promise me nobody will ever know about this, ok.

BILLY

I'm not that dumb. Thanks for the fast lesson.

GERARD

Now the jobs yours to keep you come back tomorrow and Ill get you started on your own, your stipend is primed.

BILLY

I'll be here early just for you teach.

Billy turning and vacating the cellar while Gerard ogles in vivication. Seconds later Timmy the last scheduled neophyte emerges for his lesson hurrying down to the work space, his chin length spindly black mop bouncing off his ears as he halts at the last step. Gerard quickly approaches him patting him on the right shoulder.

GERARD

I am a little fagged this afternoon already son. Sorry Timmy you can binge with your buds.

TIMMY

Oh Well Thanks I guess.

GERARD

See ya next time Timmy.

As Timmy pirouettes back up the steps Gerard reminiscing the affair with Bobby and Billy remaining turned on by their everlasting charisma. Electing to relax in a near by chair tantalizing himself in fools paradise.

GERARD REMINISCING BOBBY AND BILLYS FACES TOGETHER

Moments later picking himself up preparing to give his father word. Entering the house on the floor above to his sisters delight.

SISTER

You look starved Gerard.

SISTER 2

We are having jam and scallops

Gerard sits at the table with his family as Sister 2 slides him a dinner plate.

GERARD

Delish, thanks sis. Pop we got us two fine boys, I told them today.

DENNY

Who did you apprise Gerard surprise me.

GERARD

Bobby and Billy.

As Gerard crams his mouth full of jam.

FADE TO BLACK.

SWIMMING FOR IT ALL

Thaddeus opens his eyes into the dim morning light realizing he slept all night on the beach solo. Revoking his encounters the evening before with the old drifter and the two naked cavaliers. He sits up and goggles at the bountiful ocean, out of the corner of his eye he espies a puerile junior, probably in his late teens skittering into the water naked for a contemporary cockcrow bathing. Gawking over he waits to see if others will supervene. Nobody comes and feeling safe he stands and strolls towards the stripling suffuse with the crashing waves. The boy spots Thaddeus for the first time.

THADDEUS

Rather early for a bathing wouldn't you admit. I bet the water is quite cold still.

THE BOY

Come in with me and find out.

THADDEUS

I could use a good wake up splash this sunup.

Taking off his bedizens scrambling unveiled into the tide and wading towards the boy as he rampages Thaddeus with salt water. Thaddeus lunges at the boy submersing him. Immersing bodies in the eurybathic trend flirtatiously for a short while. The boy then jumps out elvishly sprinting towards both of their clothes picking up the piles. Thaddeus lazy realizing what was happening until the boy races down the beach with their clothes in his swaying hands.

CLOSE UP OF THE NAKED BOY SPRINTING ACROSS THE OPEN SAND CLOTHES IN HAND GLEAMING

Barreling raw Thaddeus ensues full speed catching up to the tenderfoot. Unsure if the lad was undertaking to rob him or just playing a prank he leaps at his legs twitching his ankle out from under him. Thaddeus landing on top flattening the boy deep in the sand. Restraining him with his body weight nulling any escape attempt.

THE BOY

I was just joking, I swear I wasn't going to steal from you. You caught me before I was going to throw your rags in the water for splashing me so much already.

THADDEUS

Don't lie to me you scamp I don't let anyone cheat me.

THE BOY

Fine, I'm sorry bust me.

Squirming a hook on Thaddeus's shorn testicles tugging firmly while they both lay stripped on top of one another. Thaddeus dazzled by the boys stunt he immediately fosters a boner from the rolfing.

THE BOY (CONT'D)

Will you just do me please and then let me go I promise I am not a thief.

Beaten with arousal and surprised by the proposition from such a corrupt boy Thaddeus can't resist. Aggressively stimulated and convertible the boy samples in open daylight. Thaddeus wraps up and fleetly puts his clothes back on.

THADDEUS

It's too bad I think it could of been fun walking home without my clothes. You be safe boy don't try filching the wrong pilgrim. Somebody will do you the wrong way one day. Just be careful. ok.

The boy slides his skivvies up and Thaddeus turns and tramps away.

THE BOY

All the fellows who come to this beach like to be robbed by guys like me that's why they come.

Thaddeus laughs to himself at the boys last remark and continues to traipse away revivified by the karma of the brand new day.

FADE TO BLACK.

GODS PLAN

THE MORNING SUN RISING OVER PROVIDENCE

Gordon laying asleep under his warm fluff blanket opens his eyes upon his fathers voice grumbling flagrantly.

GORDONS FATHER

Wake up, Gordon. I will not raise a coward son who is afraid to attend school. You must matriculate to be a man son. You must respect yourself enough to learn something new today.

GORDON

I'm awake damn it I have plenty of time before school starts, dad.

Gordon angrily rises and dresses remembering skipping the day before having trouble making up his mind about his plans. He steps into the kitchen where his mother stands near the dinner table.

GORDONS MOTHER

Good morning, son. I have a great breakfast for you. Let's just forget about yesterday, Gordy and eat well this morning to have a better day today for you Mother.

GORDON

Thanks Mom but I'm not hungry yet. I have something important to complete today. I don't want an upset stomach to wreck my plans.

GORDONS MOTHER

What plans, Gordon?

GORDON

Nothing I can speak of. Just something I must do for myself. I must fulfill them today. God spoke to me last night in my sleep and told me to conquer my dreams. He said to me if I fail to stand up for myself I will be a loser forever.

GORDONS MOTHER

You should not say a thing like that ever again and I forbid you to think such a thing in our home.

GORDON

I can think what I want to think, mother. God has already chosen me to do a deed to save myself today. I must not disappoint. When I come home I will be very hungry and we can have a grand dinner to celebrate.

Gordons mother smiles at her son hugs him and then kisses his forehead goodbye as he splits his home into the auroras zephyr. Strutting the ruby stone road and again omitting the path avenueing the school. Deciding to creep into the forest to knock off near the same spruce tree.

FADE TO BLACK.

BLOWN VENGEANANCE

Arising from an hours rest in the woods Gordon stares up into the teal Providence sky momentarily before standing. Reclining his mind and deciding not to think anything further his mind is made up, nothing was going to stop him. His mother's words nor his fathers threat would detour him from accomplishing God's will. Leading himself out of the woods obscurity towards the school house being careful not to be seen. Approaching the rear of the out house he stops and reposes on the lush grass behind an overgrown bush just feet from broken wood planks in the back section of the out house. Keeping a keen eye out assuring not to miss who would be taking their turn to relieve themselves. A few quick minutes elapse before a male student hurries towards Gordon first. Figuring it may be all day before he gets what he wants he totes a 7 inch blade he had tucked away in his jodhpurs and bores steadily at the sharp periphery. Sliding his pinky across the metal reach. As the male student retires back to class. Growing tired of waiting Gordon sustains cherishing his stiletto in front of him. Rolling his eyes astern in acrimony a few times.

GORDON

Where the hell is this bum.

Ten minutes drag and nobody, suddenly Gordon eavesdrops the door behind the school house slam harder then the other times and looks up. This time his prayer is answered as he locks sight on Nicholas hotfooting right at him. Pushing himself off the grass behind the bush with his free hand he discreetly skurks behind the cracked wood detecting a populous hole he can see straight inside. Nicholas opens the front door of the out house as he lets it thump behind him. Whisking his chinos down and reaching into his underwear baring himself to urinate in the malodorous hole as Gordon peeks at Nicholas's every move. Shaking off sprinkles until he's smug retaining to be exposed he starts rubbing his cock slowly then goes faster. Flabbergasted by Nicholas masturbating Gordon stares at his cock eyeballs taut against the chasm in the wood plank. Nicholas jerkin off grunting faintly then switches his hands. Gordon grips his stiletto sturdier. Clenching the wood plank with his other hand realizing this is the make or break moment he yanks back the larger plank knocking the other slabs next to it on the ground at the same time.

NICHOLAS

Get out of here!

Nicholas squeals furiously shocked and embarrassed being caught masturbating Gordon reaches at him. Clasping his penis callously with his bare palm. Vising the apex of his blade up against Nicholas's pale cheek.

GORDON

You say a word and I'll cut both your eyes out pig.

NICHOLAS

Please Gordon put that down what do you want with me. I'm sorry, please.

Gripping Nicholas's penis tensely mauling its thickness bunching in his metacarpus.

G0RD0N

You really thought you were alone. Wrong. Did you even know today's my birthday.

NICHOLAS

Is that what you want Gordon. Go for it I promise I won't tell anyone you like boys. Just keep your hand there and everything will be alright. I'll keep my mouth shut.

Reacting to Nicholas's words Gordon savagely strains his arm around his head and wraps the stilettos threshold up against the effete skin on his neck.

GORDON

If you want to take a swallow ever again you listen to me right now. Your going to show me how much you really like my pudding and when your done sucking it up you tell me how good it tastes and I'll let you live. Anything else and your fucking dead bum.

Ripping his hand off Nicholas's penis and quickly pulling his out of his worn slacks. Visibly stiff Nicholas evil eyes down at Gordon's privates.

NICHOLAS

Please Gordy I will do anything else for you. Something better I will find the prettiest girl in class for you.

GORDON

No. Last chance. You say another word and I chop your head off and start eating your brains I'm still hungry. I'm serious you squirm before I'm done and your a dead man. Get down.

Extorting the roof of Nicholas's head down to his privates uprooting his filaments with his free hand, shank still wrapped around his neck. Fearing for his life Nicholas is compelled to fornicate. Granting Nicholas a few chances to catch fresh air before he puts his mouth back to work. Placated by the sodomy Nicholas without given a fluke to take his last breath suffers a fatal kerf deep into throat. The gashing digs a massive orifice in his neck as blood sprays all over Gordons slacks. Dismembering his head pricking a deeper breach into the side of his neck. More blood squirts out infesting the out house wall. Noticing Nicholas's body going limp he holds his head up and watches the soupy cherry red blood disgorge all over Nicholas's chest. Waiting until Nicholas is entirely static he kneels to one knee. Reaching the shiv around Nicholas's shaft and without hesitation quarrying through his urethra emasculating him almost instantly. Squeezing his prize Gordon holds it up to his face poring over its glory as blood weeps off his maws. Smiling at conquering his horrific dream Gordon shoves the bloody shaft into Nicholas's own mouth. Leaning his head back against the side wall seeping fresh blood everywhere. As Nicholas's placid corpse lays perished Gordon reaches his fingers into the puddle of redness. Then spelling out the word "queen" above his head with smeared blood. Wiping his own smutted, tarnished hands clean using the shoulder part of Nicholas's school shirt. A vivid terror reigns in the breeze as self righteousness explodes in Gordons gut while he rushes out the rear of the out house towards the acroamatic woodlands.

FADE TO RED.

TOBIAS FIRST DAY

Tobias stands behind a timbered slab, three empty tumblers sit in front of him as he clouts a cruet of rum dipping it to fill the first tumbler. Sebastian reverses from the alternative side of the overblown spread facing Tobias holding a tray with four freshly dry demijohns from a table of card playing patrons. Assorted round tables host entourages of cronies and paramours bestowing scattered snickers. Sebastian strutting back to Tobias resting the demijohns near the set in front of him. Setting the tray on the bar with four exposed playing cards laying face up. Extending his hand under the bar and nimbly chafes Tobias's crotch kneading his pants. Passionately surveying his face and then back across the crammed room as cackles and prattle surround them. Tobias in gusto finishes pouring the next two tumblers as Sebastian picks up the queen of hearts from the sprawled cards and places it on the bar in front of him.

SEBASTIAN

From Daniel to you Tobias. I saw you two staring at each other earlier. Daniels a regular he comes here when he really wants to get caroused and play hard.

TOBIAS

He mentioned this was one of his favorite taverns earlier and he is so nice perhaps he merits a follow.

SEBASTIAN

Remember follow only when your comfortable Tobias this is your first night. Our tavern gets swamped, so many lechers here culling is critical.

TOBIAS

This place is great.

SEBASTIAN

It keeps getting better when your tippled to trot. Let me know if you need a break we'll take one together, okay.

TOBIAS

Okay Thanks.

Sebastian loads the refills onto his tray and leaves the bar towards the tables and waiting partisans. Daniel with his genteel potency stands and walks towards the back hallway and tavern lavatories. Tobias cases him closely making sure not to eagle eye as Daniel disappears behind a closed door. Waiting for a moment as he cleanses a tumbler with a rag then dries off his hands and follows Daniel. Remembering which door he entered Tobias pauses to gape back to see if anyone is watching him. Noticing its clear he slips in discreetly securing the door behind him.

DANIEL

No words.

Daniel mounts vanward of Tobias who appears with a analytical grin and a curious pang of eagerness about him. Daniel quickly reaches forward and covers Tobias's mouth with his right palm and steadies it breezily not saying a word. Penetrating Tobias's umber trousers squeezing him in attempts to physic a fast erection then kneels to his remedy. Revering his first carnal rapport savoring the wealth of fruition.
FADE OUT.

THE RULES OF JUSTICE

A blazing fire in the stone fireplace beacons the living headroom for Seymour as he poises pouring rum into a glass toby in front of Morgan. Sitting comfortably on a cushioned cathedra behind a wooden table, Morgan peering intently as Seymour scrupulously doctors the amount he fills for him. Stopping just as the rum edges out above an M shaped engraving nearing the top of the glass rim, smiling at Morgan and tittering for a twinkling.

SEYMOUR

Everyone who tarrys the Rose has ken all our glasses are branded for a good score.

MORGAN

Branded? You mean marked with those M's.

Morgan points to the 'M' engraving on the glass expressly.

SEYMOUR

Yes. Its bourgeois at most of the pubs like the Rose. In other colonies I know many moored drinkeries who use branded glasses like we do.

MORGAN

Why?

SEYMOUR

Well so purchasers know we own them of course. Some skates and blokes call them the M line. Some the top line or just the line. We use them to mark where to stop filling but patrons who know the game know how to read the lines.

MORGAN

How would I read the line?

SEYMOUR

Let's say your just the wino bearing cards and I'm the bartender handing you your next slug. When I cull your tables dry mugs you passed me a card. I know the card you passed was meant for me because you placed it off to the side of the tray instead of the middle. It's important you remember what I'm telling you Morgan if you are going to tend the Rose with me and the boys you must inherit the precept not just follow it.

MORGAN

How shall I remember what I haven't been told, someone owes me the proprieties of this game first.

Morgan picks up his glass and takes a healthy shwig.

SEYMOUR

Just keep paying heed please, Morgan its easy to play. When a barhand snags a players card meant for him, its on the flanking of the tray behind his taster.

Morgan slurps his rum welcoming Seymours lingo.

It matters how cushy you bustle a player at the Rose because when you wax the trays from the tables and you spot his card is a herald. You can choose to recall who sent it and query the vestige or just ignore it. Nobody can ever make you slant his card but if you want you can.

MORGAN

So tell me what does a blokes card testify for me?

SEYMOUR

I'm getting there Morgan let me explain better. So let's say you make fandangle with a guy who passes you a card. Lots of times every guy at the table passes you his card behind his taster. So its all up to you who's doodad you want to see. It's maxim that all the players can suffice cards on your salver between waiting for their next libation and grub. When they stow the card they want to requisition in the middle of the salver between tasters it is sent as harbinger for one of the guys at another table.

MORGAN

I didn't foresee this romp was going to be so hermetic.

Seymour laughs and moves around the table close to Morgan giving smooch. Putting his hand on his leg and caressing him in repose. Releasing lips warmly and obsessing Morgans eyes.

SEYMOUR

I already know your a canny enough gamin to kibitz with us at the Rose.

Continuing to toy with Morgans thigh.

SEYMOUR (CONT'D)

Now there's more for me to decree.

MORGAN

Tell me, I'm not stopping you, Seymour

SEYMOUR

There are many barflies who get soused at the Rose and don't always know how to rollick. The cunning sonnies who have played before are more popular with the lackeys. Lots of customers and the ladies who haunt the Rose think passing cards between tables is just superstition. Giving their fellow players luck by sharing cards. Believers think a man's skill rubs off and travels with each card that is wended. People give creed to peculiar things but if you aren't shrewd then passing a card is just considered superstition.

MORGAN

So am I lucky that I found you Seymour. All your skills are going to rub off on me is that what you think?

SEYMOUR

The chaps who aid the Rose possess a sleight that all the other guys want. Being the most impressive barhand isn't your only skill Morgan since your with me that makes you special.

MORGAN

I'm sure there are a lot of sly faces who come to spree at night but none will top yours.

Displaying his affection for Seymour returning a swift smooch. Seymour fingers a deck of playing cards near by.

SEYMOUR

Now Morgan there's oodles of players who also monkeyshine. A legit whim is tabbed when your keen. A king means they want you to comply to their demand. It signs they like the way your mouth moves and they are requesting you give them exactly what they want. A queen fates the same for you. When you are predestined a queen by a player, they have a kisser for you to use. You can use their chops anyway you want them.

MORGAN

My tummy is parched.

Seymour hands him a porringer rife with lavender grapes to sup.

SEYMOUR

A jack mottos the skate is requesting hand play. Some call it the joshers sign and is wild for you or him to trigger the hand play.

Seymour sliding a jack of clubs towards Morgan.

An ace is the top card to ante because it bids bounteous game and sex is the hopper. When you draw an ace from a loyal customer its the highest card he can plum. Your courting can be requited of course but usually when the ace is a spaid or club it speaks his dominance. When the ace is a heart or a diamond it coquets the customer prefers to be submissive to you.

Seymour slides two aces towards Morgan, one a red heart and the second a black spaid.

MORGAN

What is the con of the colors?

SEYMOUR

Colors ply no bilking, gents prefer a joint scene over a harry bandy. Privacy and respect is a crucial rule at our house. When times get heckled and guys get nutty for even the humblest excuses, it isn't just our job as barhands to keep the peace. Patrons make sure to quell fighting even when some don't get what they want right away there's always next time.

MORGAN

I can imagine a torrent of the elder beaus just keep playing and playing.

SEYMOUR

The frolics never quit and after hours is drollery. It's your cream who's card you ginger and there's a slew of watching at the Rose. When the time is right you can take your chance. I showed you the other day where we go, when you see your stud pay attention to the door he opens and follow. Never go in at the same time, the Rose is a bonny drinkery and card playing tavern Morgan secrecy is corporeality and no one rats.

MORGAN

Your the only one who can open my mouth Seymour.

SEYMOUR

Reputed molly houses have been burnt to the ground in London and innocent men killed when the wrong word gets out. Everybody who comes to gambol honors all the others and that is the same for you, me and the chaps who tend the Rose. Many who play and pass cards in the center of the tray are endorsing players at near by tables. There's etiquette for us movers to assent when carrying cards between tables.

MORGAN

This is becoming puzzling Seymour did somebody write the manifesto on the back pages of the bible one drunken night a thousand years ago. I wonder what colony the privy was in where he wrote it.

SEYOUR

No bible or manifesto Morgan. If you wrote down what I am telling you and gifted the scrawl to anyone in town you would be hung. God will one day accept homosexuals as equal like every other married man. No man shall pay the sooty price of a pseudo sin. Morgan I want you to be happy when your with me and when your working at the Rose always. Whenever your plaqued please tell me so I can help.

MORGAN

I think you want my help, Is it because we both have beryl eyes?

Morgan leans over and kisses Seymour beginning to take off his sark. Vellicating it over his head and on the flush ligneous floor. As Seymour does the same for Morgan and they crawl a few feet impending to the burning fire in front of them. Laying next to each other on a tweed afghan continuing their massaging. The fires crackle sheens on their bare chests and faces for a few moments before Seymour grabs the full deck of cards and watches Morgans reaction.

SEYMOUR

Signers place 3 cards in the center of your tray in front of their taster. A face card or wish card if placed properly is closest the players drink, this is his requesting curtsy. The next card placed under this card tips his seat at the table.

Sliding the ace of hearts resting on the afghan closer in front of Morgan. Seymour rests his rum in front of the ace then pulls a 10 of diamonds and sets it just below the ace.

SEYMOUR (CONT'D)

The second card if it is a 10 it signs he is sitting at the north seat of the table.

Seymour grabs a 2 of clubs from the deck and replaces the 10 with it under the ace.

SEYMOUR (CONT'D)

A 2 cues the player is sitting at the south end.

Again reaching into the deck Seymour plucks a 6 of spaids substituting the 2.

SEYMOUR (CONT'D)

A 6 clues the player is sitting at the west seat of table.

Next grabbing a 4 of hearts ousting the 6.

SEYMOUR (CONT'D)

So this leaves the 4 to gesture the player sitting at the seat to the east. When a boob passes a card which is not a 2,4,6, or 10 that means he made a blunder which is always his gaffe. He doesn't know the precedents or he is throwing a comment card to a friend or foe. All other cards passed which don't tip the players seat at the table are considered comment cards.

MORGAN

Always knowing the direction can be handy I see. What do the comment cards mecca? One number could have a lot more then one thing to say.

SEYMOUR

There are no bona fide comments dubbed for certain numbered cards. Versed grifters use buzz cards that mean disparate things to different people. Some good friends playing in the same room know how to read the comments because they've played together before and both know what the number card stands for. Swindlers will tell you one thing to listen to with these comment cards and other guys will tell you the opposite, Who you harken to is all up to you.

MORGAN

This third card what does is it fortune?

SEYMOUR

The third card is also either a 10,2,6, or 4 which destines the seat the jade is sitting in he intends to sign. He wants you to be a tip top hand and pass his signs. Up to snuff bar hands must supplant the cues because they want to succeed entree to the right person. So when you pick up a full tray of empty tasters and cards both in the center of the tray and flanking for you. When flipping them and filling the glasses you have time to realize who's who and what you pine.

MORGAN

My heads going to roll if I flub.

SEYMOUR

You'll catch on fast and there's a luxury of lushers to crave. When a gent playing cards at the Rose sets his 3 cards in the middle of our tray for you to pass that means the grind is ordained.

MORGAN

Seems a crafty gig to ploy, a lot of corners to lift and tipple to ante.

SEYMOUR

In deed yes. When players parlay 3 cards with their drink and they know the game. Score whos face card slanted him and where he's sitting. When this clicks he can do whatever he wants with the nod, keeping the cards next to him at the table. When sharing and sending flash cards they are always used from a second deck. Players call it the party deck and anyone who wants to play the game must own his own party deck to pass cards.

MORGAN

I think you party too much Seymour. Your so drunk right now your just making this all up to get arouse out of me.

SEYMOUR

The only rouse you are going to get is when you wake up with me tomorrow and still remember the rules. The way I taught you them tonight and your life will only keep getting better and better every night.

MORGAN

Every night I am with you or every night I am helping the boys at the Rose?

SEYMOUR

Both let me prove everything is the way fate wants you to want it to be.

MORGAN

Fate is so confusing my mother told me fate is the gate to heavens door that it sees through the cracks of time to show me Gods way. My father once told me fate is destiny and the only way I can live to see my destiny is if I listen to God. He also told me the devil will try to speak to me one day and lead me down the path of sin and early death. That I must ignore his gambit to steal my soul and go my own way. You know what I told him.

SEYMOUR

What did you tell him?

MORGAN

I told my father how do I know that one day isn't today. What if following God's word is the trick of the devil. I wouldn't know either way until after I die.

SEYMOUR

Life's trick is staying alive long enough to trust yourself. Morgan I want you to know you can always trust me and our secrets are not sins. God remains with all men who truly trust each other and themselves.

MORGAN

You know what else I remember about that day I spoke to my dad. It was the first time I ever told him I loved him.

SEYMOUR

You don't have to tell me all of this Morgan but I love you for it I do.

MORGAN

I love you too.

Seymour picks up Morgans glass for him handing it to him and grabs his own holding it near Morgans.

SEYMOUR

A toast to getting drunk, to love, to all the house rules you just learned, to fate and destiny, to trust, and to the devils trick we just found out together tonight.

Morgan and Seymour toast each other finishing their rum.

SEYMOUR (CONT'D)

There is only one more thing you need to know.

MORGAN

Enlighten me.

SEYMOUR

The engravings on our glasses at the Rose, they are used to serve our answer. For the bar hands like you and I who own the game. When you fill a glass to the very top of this marking or above it this shows him your swallow to his wish card. What happens next is a game of waiting and following. I think you know what I mean.

MORGAN

Now I know why nobody minds that drinking so much makes them to need to use the wash rooms so many times every night.

SEYMOUR

When you don't fill the customers glass above the peak of this highwater mark but it is satisfied between the engravings bottom edge and its top. This proves your interest is sincere but the time isn't right. The time can't be right for everybody at the same time, do you copy Morgan?

MORGAN

I catch ya, time is just one big lark.

SEYMOUR

When you fill the customer to the bottom edge of the fix or even visibly below this bottom groove this attests your not interested. It doesn't mean you give up on the gent forever you always confess the chance to change your mind his next refill. For these hard luck gents it just isn't their night. No big deal obviously there's always more losers then winners playing cards at their tables anyway.

MORGAN

I'm not that crude, I love to see the hoary gents smile too.

Morgan chuckles and reaches over to rub Seymours leg as the two idolizers roll over together compressing exposed teats as the burning fire pops.

FADE OUT.

PARLOUR ROOM PROPOSITION

SUN SETTING OVER BOSTON

Zac and Jacob pop in the rear entrance of the flophouse occupied by habitue. Jacob approaching an elevated wooden countertop in the parlour room with a myriad of brimming vials stashed on a motley of mantles on the wall behind him.

JACOB

Time to romp, my head needs fixed.

Standing buoyantly behind the counter is short ochre haired, bewitching Seth hosting for the nighttripping with Josh and Terry, who are engaged in a card game at a table in front of the bar with two older patrons.

SETH

Look what they brought in for us this morning.

Seth pointing around the corner at a novel billiards table into the abutting expanse as an assemblage of carousel peons tackle a game of billiards.

ZAC

This joint is so rowdy without that now it's going to be bedlam.

Scott and Samuel sauntering from the expanse accost Jacob and Zac.

SCOTT

Our take is going to hike with those balls banging.

POOL BALLS EXPLODING OFF A BREAK

A loutish throng of drunkards surround the billiards table grasping stoups of beer in tomfoolery as the pool balls are played.

HALLWAY DOOR SHUTTING

Bearish and bewhiskered 31 year old Spencer pulls Zac's rawboned body close towards him engrossing both his shoulders simultaneously with his paws.

SPENCER

Remember what I told you Zac, nobody can know of us. You cure me now and join me Saturday for a fair split of our spoils. Perhaps your bud Jacob can annex with our quarry.

Accepting Spencers offer Zac turns to face the shabby wall inside the discreet, bantam room. Sliding his effete trousers to knee level, clenching his palms around Zac's glossy buttocks Spencer esteems his pride.

ZAC

This booty best be sterling.

FADE TO BLACK.

SHIRTS OFF

The cardinal room of the White Rose, One thirty a.m. chock with strapping beaus the card games continue deep into the night. Cocky with peerless groomed champagne hair and a teeming mouth, touching his own intimidatingly suntanned, bulging teats Charles brags tigerishly and dares the others near him sitting at the table.

CHARLES

The next butterfly who comes back in here from whizzing gets to pick the best looking.

MORGAN

The swain he chooses receives a meal and drinks all night compliments the Rose.

25 year old 6 foot 4 and paper thin sable haired Craig boasts to the guild.

CRAIG

Charles, since your so cavalier around us chaps why has your bravado failed to marry a gilded squaw.

CHARLES

This pub is for us suitors but where are all the hardy gamin? Most of you lads are skimpy, I want to find the sturdy players.

Two trite men return from the wash room back into the cardinal room as the modest of the two is grabbed by Craig and crew.

CRAIG

This yokel is splendid to honor us a winner. Gents shirts off and make a line.

Fifteen stripped beaus form a line next to each other as Craig rests his arm around the scrawny man, pausing to judge meticulously. Staring at the posse of tight bellies surmising, everyone at the tables is crooning and spawning obscene melodies from their cupped mouths. Enticed by Charles's savvy dark tan and chiseled chest the scrawny man points him out as winner. Charles reacting brashly and raising both arms up flexing his golden muscles for the aroused mob. Claps and hurrahs monopolize the room as Morgan jaunts towards Charles resting a glutted plate of potatoes in front of the espoused champ.

PHILLY STYLE

Elderly white whiskered and pleasantly chubby big wig known as Stanley rambles into the airy mid afternoon pub near downtown Philadelphia off of Chestnut street. Sebastian and Tobias are serving with confrere bar hands Elijah and Justin, both 19. Flourishing similar brusque nut brown hair and with lusty smiles snickering before observing Stanley seated forlorn, he is the only man in the tavern besides them. A humble bevy of callow chaps had just exited as Stanley popped in.

ELIJAH

What can we boys get for you today, sir?

STANLEY

A syllabub to tidy my mind, thanks.

Justin fills a glass mug resting it in front of him as Stanley gazes past a cranny in his polo. Craving to see more flesh Stanley belts his syllabub. Tobias briskly refilling him as he tosses half and sets it on the bar sinking back to relax.

STANLEY (CONT'D)

Boys I know the rumors are true some scuttlebutt surfaced in the hall about your hostelry again. I won't ever let this tavern perish from any hoax. I tell you what I am longing all four of you lads together this time, if you shall remedy an old man to ease his marbles. Go in the back washroom and get adjusted for me together. I'll seal the doors and be right back to cool you off. I'm going to show you boys your always protected.

Sebastian acknowledging Stanley's request and honoring his status with the tavern he leads Tobias, Elijah and Justin into the far washroom candidly. Elijah resting his arm around Tobias's shoulders while Justin surprises Sebastian with a snappy kiss. Shutting the front door closing the tavern momentarily Stanley recedes to the rear where his tender cohorts are eager receiving him. Stanley bleeding to his knees to Justins succor getting him hard in an instant. Elijah and Tobias divvy a smooch while Sebastian joins in the luxury. Stanley swaps benefits to Tobias then pronto to Elijahs favor. Sebastian gracing the scene with a snug smile.

SEBASTIAN

Protect us. Whore!

Twirling Stanleys pearly curls with his fingers Sebastian aids Stanley's dunking face. Tobias reaching his digit gingerly into Sebastians mouth dogging him in fetish. Elijah crouching and unbottoning Stanley's trousers for him as Justin squats to godsend his pundit.

STANLEY

Their jealous backbiting about you boys won't be condoned at assembly anymore. I promise to bear auspice for all partisans of your pub. I'll have all your backs no matter what some of those married nitwits sham.

TOBIAS

We all love you Stanley.

GASPEE BURNING

June 9th, 1772 Narraganset Bay off the coast of Warwick, Rhode Island. British customs schooner HMS Gaspee chasing the packet ship Hannah clanks brutaly on rock bottom in shallow water. Lieutenant Dudinston atop ships deck bellowing in tirade at his corps.

LIETENANT DUDINSTON

You bums are feeding us to the rats get this ship free!

Ashore a band of raucous colonists guffaw and eyeball the watery scene. At the break of dawn a kinship of nihilists paddle their gondola across the cursory bay current. Gallantly boarding the Gaspee in blaring whoopee as a gunshot tolls and Lieutenant Dudinston's legs tumble. In jibe to looting and the crew plunging deck vast flames ravish the schooner to waterline.

FLAMES RAZING THE GASPEE

The rebels flee paddling promptly to shore parading the bounty. A British flag is ditched in scows center, circling it unbottoning their breeches in coalescent faddism screeching and peeing taunting English menace.

FADE TO BLACK.

AN ASS FOR AN ARROW

Traipsing the pebbly Watauga river banks red headed Drake and favorite cuz Jonah barefooting far from their parents hamlet. Bypassing the treatied frontier into Cherokee land unknowingly they stop for a lay down break at rivers edge.

JONAH

Shall we take a nude bathing this morning. My body needs a good washing, come on Drake.

DRAKE

My skin aches for a bathing.

As they both toss off their clothing plunging into the shallow creek water. Trampling in knee deep water and then further until they stand aside one another in the shoulder length creek water near center. Splashing each other for a moment before dunking their heads under together relishing the bathing. Lasting a few minutes before walking to shore and plopping down naked near their clothes. Jonah lays back with hands behind his head first as Drake follows.

JONAH

My father taught me gods lesson from the sun can only truly be learned by a nude body. It feels good out here today.

Shot from behind a cluster of bushes fifty feet behind them a wooden arrow with a sharpened three inch arrowhead jolts into the ground between the two undraped boys. Drake turns and faces the bushes spotting two Cherokee Indians brandishing crossbows and arrows clamoring in evanescent indian jibe.

CHEROKKE INDIAN

Leave our land now! These waters do not belong to you whites! Leave!

Jonah and Drake thrusting to their feet as fast as possible Drake grabbing both of their clothes as they sprint away alongside the creek towards their parents village. As they reach fifty feet from where they lay a second arrow is shot striking Jonah in his right buttocks. Ebbing hard to the ground Drake fastly helps him recover to his feet staring at his wound dribbling blood down his buttocks and the back of his right leg.

DRAKE

We must keep going before they kill us! Hurry!

Embracing Jonah with his left arm wrapped around his torso and Jonahs right arm around Drakes neck struggling to scurry away from the frenzied Indians. Finally resting behind a vast oak tree Jonah tends his wound yanking the arrow entirely out of his slit flesh. Snapping it in half over his left knee in grimace.

JONAH

They are going to pay for what they've done to me.

FADE OUT.

A TEA PARTY TO ATTEND

December 16th, 1773, the streets circumscribing the Old South meeting house in downtown Boston are compact with thousands of raucous colonists bellowing piercingly and crooning anthems of "No taxation without representation". Inside the meeting house is jarringly uproaring and in the front row is Jacob next to his father Jamie bawling as a paunchy, spry Samuel Adams is giving spiel. Zac is standing to the other side of Jacob also next to his father Don scorning with the horde. Near by is Cuddy, Scott and their father James conforming to buffoonery.

CLOSE UP OF SAMUEL ADAMS FACE IN IDIOM RECITING "THIS MEETING CAN DO NOTHING MORE TO SAVE THE COUNTRY"

Much of the rebellious rabble disbands the scene into the streets towards Griffin's wharf and the British tea ships. Jacob, Zac, Cuddy and Scott rendezvous with their fathers in a justled second story abode where Jack, Eban, Charles and fellow cohorts of the Sons of Liberty are present. Jack and Eban are finger painting red war paint on each others noses, cheeks and forehead. Charles affixes feathers behind his ears and then aiding Zac with paint on his face aiding in warrior disguise. Jacob parodies his chest with coloring and feathers in his hair symbolizing a Mohawk indian. The room is clamorous with rebel chants as the clan prepares to affranchise the colonies with a forte act of sedition.

THE TRIBE OF PATRIOTS DRESSED AS MOHAWK INDIANS BOARD THE BRITISH SHIPS 'DARTMOUTH', 'ELEANOR' AND 'BEAVER' DUMPING TEA INTO THE BOSTON HARBOR

FADE TO RED.

LIFTING CORNERS

Inside a crushed New York tavern as a multitude of assiduous card games prosper. Seymour poised behind the bar in process of resting a tray rife with tasters and cards on the slab. Clasping a brimming pitcher of beer pouring the tasters chockablock to the intaglios with one hand and lifting the corners of endorsed cards with his other. Appraising his luck he focuses across the parlour room to a cherished caller.

CLOSE UP OF SEYMOURS THUMB LIFTING CORNERS AND FOCUSING IN ON HIS CHERISHED CALLER AS HE STANDS SAUNTERING TO A REAR WASH ROOM

FADE OUT.

BEER SOP

Four dipsomaniac patrons consuming and concluding a hand lob their cards towards the center of the table together. The three losers simultaneously pick their mugs up and bombard the winner with their beer inundating him instantly.

CLOSE UP OF THE WINNERS FACE DRIBBLING COLD BEER AS HE DODDERS IN IRONY

Sebastian ambles to the soaked scene holding a fresh ewer of brewski.

SEBASTIAN

You quacks never said it was bath time.

Scoffing the drenched provocateur dumps the choate ewer of brewski over his head as suds roll down his face to a dexter guffawing around the room.

A ROOM FULL OF DIPSOMANIACS REACT MIMICING SEBASTIANS LEVITY DOUSING THEIR HEADS WITH THEIR BREW IN COINCIDENCE

FADE OUT.

RIDING THE BOOTY

An eerie still of calignosity surrounds Zac, Jacob, Josh, Terry, Spencer and his crony Jeff. All donning twill disguises with holes cut out for their eyes and mouth over their heads. Conniving in the posterior of a covered wagon as it comes to an impasse near a wooden fence bordering a private field permeated with scattered mustang.

JEFF

I refuse to die with you dupes. You catch your colt and you all know where we unite.

SPENCER

Good luck, donkey boys.

Josh leaps from the covered wagon first as the piratic moiety hop fence giving chase through the gloaming.

THE SIX BANDITS RIDE THEIR BOOTY LIONIZING THROUGH THE DARK

FADE TO BLACK.

FIRST CONTINENTAL CONGRESS

September 5th, 1774 Philadelphia, Pennsylvania inside Carpenters hall an inconoclast assembly of delegates from twelve colonies are mooting over the coercive acts. Patrick Henry stands to pitch his notions.

PATRICK HENRY

Every colony shall be in concord with a novel system where boycott and repeal is our inimitable resolution.

A prominent bisection of optimism replicas throughout the hall.

JOHN JAY

Rescission of these intolerable acts is an irrefutable comeuppance.

John Adams claps miming the moxie of his dictum.

FADE OUT.

POWDER ALARM

A cellar crammed with stocked barrels loaded with gun powder is in process of becoming steeped deeper as a fraternity of junior patriots abet each other hoisting the impervious powder into place. 13 year old Cory erects at the mouth of the cellar gorged by the sunlight behind him, grabbing the crotch of his breeches with his legs spread.

CORY

Any loyalist swine who sees me with our stash down here, can just suck it.

CORY SQUEEZING THE BULGE OF HIS BREECHES CASTING A SHADOW INTO THE CELLAR

FADE TO BLACK.

THADDEUS JOINS THE PARTY

Thaddeus and Seymour pace side by side down the cobblestone boulevard outside the White Rose barging in virtuously and approach Christopher and Garret smirking behind the bar. Seymour nods to his pals and briskly introduces Thaddeus as new help before accompanying him to aft most wash room.

SEYMOUR

Ever matinee an orgy?

Muscling the door ajar and championing Thaddeus inside full tilt. Morgan and Todd are sheered in dandle. The four admirers eyeball then foretaste in felicity.

MORGAN

Welcome to heaven.

FADE OUT.

GUNSMITH GUNG HO

Gerard reposed atop a crate replete with brand new muskets contrived in his fathers basement workshop. Bartering with robust 28 year old gunsmith Daryl for quittance over his guns. He brandishes a rifle showing if off for a flash then handing it to Daryl before bidding farewell. Daryl hefts the crate to the corner of the room as 16 year old apprentice Kenny busts in on time for instruction. Scraggy and engendering girlish long tufts Kenny advances towards his mentor. Daryl retreats to the door and jams a near by rifle into the slot blocking access into the clearance. Wielding his protracted musket aiming it at Kenny turbulently.

DARYL

My chandler spoke of you as a phony Kenny. Prove to me you aren't some butch hussy and drop your drawers for me. Convince me you are packing heat and not some pussy.

Stupefied by the premise Kenny doesn't hesitate to drop his drawers striving to verify his masculinity.

Daryl lowers his rifle pointing it at Kenny's raw brawn snickering in paradox.

FADE OUT.

REVERE'S RIDE

April 18th, 1775 a neoteric night tide overwhelming the north end Boston neighborhood as a pudgy, eccentric Paul Revere lurches on his horse disappearing towards the Charles River. Nearby dallying in a courtyard en route Zac and Josh scurry from necking behind a series of exorbitant bushes as Paul speeds by them.

JOSH

You in a hurry for anything particular, old man?

PAUL

The regulars are coming out.

REVERE RIDING BRISKLY IN THE TWILIGHT AND THEN ROWING ACROSS THE CHARLES RIVER DISCREETLY

Continuing his ride north through Middlesex county warning colonists on the way as bells are rung, drums tolled, bonfires lit and trumpets gigged to warn the country folk the British are coming. Paul arriving in Lexington flush at midnight.

JOHN HANCOCK AND SAMUEL ADAMS OPENING THE FRONT DOOR WELCOMING PAUL REVERE INSIDE WITH HIS MESSAGE

FADE OUT.

LEXINGTON

A militia of intrepid rebels lined up in the Lexington green at dawning stand their ground as an outnumbered throng of red coats arrive instigating demoralization chanting "Huzzah" at the rebels. Crouched gutsily proximate Buckman tavern an apostle for the revolution fires a single shot above the British troops. Simultaneously a colonial prisoner is shot and killed fleeing for his freedom by a British regular. Mayhem ignites as the rebels disperse into the woods and behind walls in midst of a deadly volley from the subordinate red coats. Inside Buckman tavern a curious teenager takes a mouthful of barley pop leftover from a mug at the bar then hustles out the door engaging a coterie of renegade teenage on lookers in the street as the fracas ensues.

THE REBELS DISPERSING INTO THE WOODS AS BRITISH TROOPS FIRE UPON THEM

FADE OUT.

CONCORD AND METONOMY

Colonial revolutionaries hasten to assemble on Punkatasset hill near the north bridge in Concord. The British cross the north bridge from the other side of the water as pandemonium emanates. Bodies fall and shots splash into the Concord river. While enemy lines gaze across the river and the British occupy the bridge a mentally ill drunkard known as Elias Brown stalks both sides in attempts to sell hard cider to the combatting soldiers.

SMOKE RISING FROM THE BURNING IN VILLAGE SQUARE AS BRITISH TROOPS DISCHARGE CONCORD MARCHING TO CHARLESTOWN

Hours later in Metonomy, Jacob, Zac, Cuddy, Eban, Jack, Charles, Josh, Terry, Soott, Robert, and Samuel with the company of their insurgent fathers course into position behind stone blockades near a tavern. Patrons bustle into the taverns basement to take cover from an onslaught of British fire. The marching troops are in sight as the minutemen returning a hail of bullets. Jacob and Zac blip shoulders in reparation after witnessing aimed regulars fall. With the confederacy of their fathers, friends and fellow minutemen they retreat into the safety of the woods sharing volley with the approaching army. Inside the tavern two inebriated scalawags prevail together at a table chugging their last potation. Without hesitation mistaking the drunks as rebels British soldiers lay them fatal target.

SLOW MOTION OF THE TWO DRUNKARDS FALLING TO THE TAVERN FLOOR MORTALLY WOUNDED

FADE TO RED.

A REVOLUTION AUTHORED

May 10th, 1775 the second continental congress convenes in Philadelphia with the new arrivals of John Hancock and Benjamin Franklin.

TABLES FILLED WITH DELEGATES AS PARLEY PROPAGATES

The same day led by patriots Ethan Allen and Benedict Arnold, the green mountain boys cross lake Champlain in Vermont and seize Fort Ticonderoga from British control.

GREEN MOUNTAIN BOYS PLUNDERING LIQUOR AND PROVISIONS FROM THE SEIZED FORT

A brotherhood of Americans ritualizing the occasion slosh the plundered liquor in unity.

FADE OUT.

FATHERS LEGACY AT BUNKER HILL

June 17th, 1775 on Breeds Hill in Boston, Americans in picket of looming British forces rabbleroused with an onslaught of fire reciprocate with spunk as crippled soldiers flail. Jacobs father Jamie arm to arm with Zac's father Don surge unflinchingly yielding bayonets at the archenemies in red coats. Striking an assailing soldier with the end of his bilbo Jamie maneuvers toward another in sync with Don who stabs an adversary sternly. Abruptly pronged in the back Don ebbs to the grass rolling a few feet down the hill. Jamie reacting to defend his fallen compatriot in attempts to drag him to asylum is purloined his livelihood by antithesis sword.

JAMIES BALEFUL WOUND BUDGES HIM FORWARD ON TOP OF DONS DEAD BODY AS THE TWO FATALLY BRANDED REVOLUTIONARIES LAY FACE TO FACE

The next mornings sun deflects off Jacob and Zac's skin as they enrapture one another in lingering embrace consoling their father's death in battle.

JACOB

We shall gather to be our own family, you and I. Rapture without tit for tat we will boast, our dads have died for us to plume.

FADE TO BLACK.

NEW YEARS HOMEAGE

The last seconds in countdown to 1776 is extolled by jagged sycophants in the avenues surrounding the New York taverns where Seymour and Morgan tend the adornment. Todd, Garret, Brad, Paul, Stephen, Timmy and devotees of the Rose poise in warble brandishing elixirs rejoicing.

MARSHALED IN REGALE THE BOYS CLAMOR IN PSALM HALLOWING 1776

FADE OUT.

COMMON SENSE AND NATURAL LIBERTY

January 1776, house by house sweeping across the colonies reveling in revolt, sympathizers ruminate the ideas of natural liberty and freedom from English rule. Published in the pamphlet titled 'Common Sense' for thousands of colonist to flip.

COMMON REBEL AFICIONADOS FLIPPING THE PAGES OF 'COMMON SENSE' IN VIVRE OF THE MOVEMENT FOR LIBERTY

FADE OUT.

BRITISH EVACUATE BOSTON

Steeped atop a tilted cannon Zac with legs spread and flinging slides down the thick metal howitzer landing on both feet. A guild of gloating patriots in salvo to the British evacuating Dorchester Heights and the port of Boston.

A FRATERNITY OF AMERICANS CHEERING THE EVACUATION

FADE OUT.

TIME FOR INDEPENDENCE

July 4th, 1776 inside Independence Hall in Philadelphia, John Hancock is the first to sign the declaration ratifying an au courant country.

JOHN HANCOCK SIGNING THE DECLARATION OF INDEPENDENCE

July 8th, the liberty bell is rung loud announcing the reading of the declaration as a wild crowd of onlookers circle the orator. During confabulation Stanley spots Sebastian and Tobias in the conflux converging them nonchalantly. The three of them disperse into a near by tavern as Stanley confides a proposal for them to stint as spies for the continental army. Rationalizing to them they shall carrot from their enterprise. Sebastian and Tobias cordially welcoming the contingency. Stanley walks them to stables a few blocks away and acquaints them with the frosted ponies they will be riding and their incipient missions ahead.

STANLEY

This coming weekend the grandiose soiree we are gilding must be august. The many lionized nihilists frequenting our party will oblige your talents.

SEYMOUR

We are glad our forte will be desired, for our lands liberty is a supreme cause.

FADE OUT.

BEHEADING FROM THE MOB

July 9th, New York City. The first reading of the declaration has just concluded and a rambunctious mob of benefactors rush down Broadway street stampeding into the bowling green and begin sawing down a fence bordering the equestrian statue of King George III. Prevailed by shepherds of the Sons of Liberty and by Seymour, Morgan and concomitants who squire in the demolishing and beheading of the gargantuan statue.

KING GEORGE 111'S DECAPITATING HEAD ATOP A STAKE IN THE GROUND NEIGHBORING THE WHITE ROSE PUB

FADE OUT.

LIBERTY SOIREE AND CABAL TO VAUNT

Chestnut street in downtown Philadelphia holding carnival to lavish bash as the popular pubs lining the acclaimed avenue are plethoric with zealots gobbling and tippling to diversion. Having arrived from New York the same day Seymour, Morgan and companions agog to accost beauteous wooers. Jacob and Zac having entertained the trip to Philadelphia from Boston with Cuddy, Eban, and Jack are sipping mimbos and whistle bellies with the legion of carousers in the street and a multitude of pubs. Including the hostelry and saloon Sebastian and Tobias lay grindstone. Standing and supping spirits chortling Zac catches Tobias's eye instantly seduced by his swank looks he chooses to solicit his company with bombos in hand for him and Jacob.

TOBIAS

Perhaps you two strapping lads would like to bang a game of cricket with me and Seymour in back.

ZAC

Sure, sounds like a rumpus, I am Zac by the way and my buddy is Jacob we are here from Boston.

SEBASTIAN

We welcome you fellows to our brouhaha, we are ordained to pamper.

Tobias and Sebastian chaperon Zac and Jacob to the grassy area behind their saloon where a cricket match has already begun. Beating them to the clambake is Seymour, Morgan, Todd and Garret. Seymour in half dishabille topless flexing his abs for his shrilling chums while Morgan disrobes his trousers into his jockeys in repercussion to losing the match. The eight glamorous bachelors coincide eye contact for the first time divvying bedazzlement.

SEYMOUR

How splendid of you skates to coalesce with us. Do you condole a match?

Esteeming the motion Tobias, Sebastian, Zac and Jacob engage the New Yorkers in a crusade of high jinx which lasts for hours. Coddling personalities and cherishing each others boody while lapping bombos, rattle-skulls and syllabubs. Todd and Garret disclosing plans to sail to England to tend Todd's grandfathers pub in Liverpool. Requisitioning to collect bountiful capital to return to the colonies and open their own alehouse together.

SEBASTIAN

One day I fancy us a resort on the coast where we can grace and savor each other for eternity without the everyday drudgeries of our pubs.

MORGAN

I second that notion, a fantastic hub with perks. Frills our city taverns can't sponsor.

JACOB

Such a sumptuous ocean side estate you are dreaming of I believe I can effectuate for us all to retire too soon enough.

ZAC

Do you speak of that dying old man Phillip Burns, the buccaneer skipper with all those tobacco fields on the New Jersey coast?

JACOB

Mr. Burns in deed, I have been privileged to be company to his libertinism and told it was in his avidity I secede to inherit his wealth and dominion if I so consent. When he croaks of course but that sudden moirai may impel any day now.

SEBASTIAN

Such a wheel of fortune would stir my consent.

JACOB

I fathom you only the truth and promise I shall send forth reverent invitations to each of you zippy chaps the day I reckon word and ride to New Jersey myself.

TOBIAS

Quite a doughty feeler from such a sassy courter if I may so admit.

The newfound paramours acquiesce the surreal scenario slurping more flips and stonewalls into the dusk. Todd and Garett depart early to rendezvous with a pal of his grandfathers. Jacob, Zac, Seymour,

Morgan, Sebastian and Tobias raise tasters for a toast giving blessing to the stalwart proposal.

THE SIX BLESSED CONFRERES RAISING TASTERS GIVING TOAST

FADE OUT.

GREAT FIRE OF NYC

September 21st, 1776 as an effusion of brilliant flames encompass a portion of lower Manhattan and city dwellers flee for their safety.

FADE TO RED.

FAMOUS LAST WORDS

The next day inside a steamy wash room in the rear of the Dove Tavern on Post road two suppliants are cosseting as a blatant knock thumps through the door bollixing their shtick. Swiftly skedaddling the wash room Morgan and a burgeoning son Felix amble to the scene outside. Catching their attention is a stunning 21 year old named Nathan Hale being escorted to Park of Artillery abut the Dove tavern. There they espy an adolescent African American slave help tighten the noose around Nathan's neck allowing him a brief moment for his last words.

NATHAN

I only regret for I have but one life to give for my country.

Disenchantingly they watch the handsome spy being hanged for his malfeasance.

MORGAN

I must escape this atrocity, Felix ride with me tonight to tryst with Seymour in Albany. A safe haven sits pretty for us there in the country.

MORGAN AND FELIX RIDE A STEED THROUGH THE STARRY NIGHT

FADE TO BLACK.

A CHRISTMAS PRESENT FROM FATE

December 25th, 1776 9 miles north of Trenton, New Jersey commander in chief of the American armies George Washington surveys the icy conditions of the Delaware river. Electing an elaborate and dangerous crossing in order to surprise the Hessians camped in Trenton on Christmas night.

GEORGE WASHINGTON SLIPPING WAIST DOWN INTO FREEZING WATER CROSSING THE DELAWARE RIVER WITH HIS MILITA

A successful crossing embarks a cold hike into Trenton in bizarre conditions for Washington's men as they attack a sleeping and ill prepared fleet of Hessians who surrender most of their force.

FADE OUT.

A FINANCIERS POTLUCK

The next day standing and summoning the pilot of a American pirate ship ashore the Delaware river in Philadelphia is financier and acclaimed politician Robert Morris. Steering his bounty of war supplies from France into the proper locale Robert is satisfied after paying the captain for the loot. He retreats to his posh homestead for a grand potluck with his visiting orphan bambinos.

A DINNER TABLE REPLETE WITH POMPOUS SELECTION OF MEATS AND DESERTS IS SET FOR ROBERT AND HIS TWO ORPHAN COMPANIONS

Sitting across from each other are two chintzy male orphans who are visiting Robert for dinner and the evening together rewarded for their good behavior at the orphanage. Surprising the two orphans by appearing from his knees from under the table near Robert to a standing position is 18 year old abecedarian servant Ronnie with shaggy brown quills and a tasteful smirk he takes a seat next to his master. Robert sparkling in his everyday ponderous posture endows a smile at Ronnie.

ROBERT

Shall commander Washington and all his brave men receive their deserved perquisite, ay men.

FADE OUT.

PRINCETON PROVES THE PARLEY

January 3rd, 1777 Princeton, New Jersey is the landscape as George Washington sparks his militia to victory over the British as the last soldiers surrender inside Nassau Hall conceding the American cause.

NEW RECRUITS ENLISTING IN THE GROWING AMERICAN ARMY

FADE OUT.

FROSTED PONIES

SIDE BY SIDE THE WHITE PONIES RIDE

Sebastian and Tobias ride their peppy frosted white ponies side by side through the daylight in quest to gain position to spy the impending British troops in the countryside near Chadds Ford, Pennsylvania. Waiting up till the haze of dusk before catching glimpse of the marching red coats the two idolizer spies pause in trot to lean over and give smooch and dandle while remaining on their sanctified ponies then riding off through the twilight to alert Commander Washington of the Brits position.

FADE TO BLACK.

PAYING FOR THE PRICE OF SIN

Zac, Jacob, Josh and Terry wearing fur masks over their head and obfuscous attire sneak through an open window of an affluent Boston merchant. Unaware him and his wife are upstairs the desperados ransack the opulent home seeking commodities to traffic on the black market. Hearing the clatter downstairs the homeowners scurry from their bedroom to witness the robbery quickly Terry hasps the married couple with rope. Aided in the tying of the ropes and covering of their heads with a bag Josh fastens them to separate dining room chairs unable to see their perpetrators. After filling the plunderage in knapsacks all the scofflaws except Jacob return to Spencer and Jeff tarrying in a covered wagon outside the home ready to scoot. Jacob dawdles for a few last words to his patsies.

JACOB

Although we have purloined all your wares I want you to know we are not an omen from any beezlebub. Jacob carefully unbuttons the merchants britches as he squirms and murmurs fashioning him a posey until copulation. Leaving his wife untouched Jacob absconds from the home joining his disciples in escaping.

FADE TO BLACK.

GLORY IN ALBANY

September 11th, 1777 at Brandywine creek the American army suffers a setback after hours of mortiferous fighting tableaus a bloody diorama. Days later in Germantown another misfortune causes a messenger to notify Sebastian and Tobias their avail is coveted in Saratoga, New York. As they ride their esteemed ponies into Albany to the hermitage occupied by Seymour and Morgan. There they are given refuge and sustenance from their hunky allies. Bestowing American General Horatio Gates with tactical assuefaction from spying on the enemies Sebastian and Tobias anticipate the aftermath of the fighting at Saratoga. Cooling off by sharing piquant libations and stories with Seymour and Morgan, word of the British's surrender arrives on October 17th.

BURGOYNES OFFICIAL SURRENDER TO GATES AT THE BATTLE OF SARATOGA

The day after the American victory at Saratoga the asylum dualing as a drinkery for exalted soldiers is discovered by a cadre of spoony blossoming infantrymen. A section of the bar is deployed for the libinous young men to rally kicks through the assuage of circular holes manicured in the wooden walls below waist level. A plank is slid out of the way exposing the holes to be used for the randy infantrymens glory as Felix and lascivious bar hand Alex are plopped on their knees before the holes galvanizing the soldiers in turn. Morgan remedies their thirst with blackstraps and bogus as Seymour, Tobias and Sebastian tend to the hankering of the young men. Oft times swapping positions with Felix and Alex and aiding in refilling hootch for the clientele.

FADE OUT.

WASHINGTONS CRAVING

On December 18th, 1777 a courier for the American army delivers an epistle from George Washington himself to Tobias and Sebastian desiring their courtesy to attend his quarters in Valley Forge for winter encampment. Admiring the request they leave the hermitage and their cohorts guaranteeing to reunite in the future.

TOBIAS AND SEBASTIAN RIDING OFF ON THEIR WHITE PONIES

Arriving frazzled from the journey to Valley Forge, George Washington salutes his solicited sojourners cordially. Blazoning to them his ambitions and furnishing them with a scrumptious supper and slumber time parlance.

GEORGE WASHINGTON

Boys I want you to know I hold your reputation in high regard and honor our confidentiality. My craving for your fitness is elite and your time with me this winter shall be liquidated supremely.

Tobias and Sebastian share a snigger with the Commander.

WASHINGTON NAKED UNDER BLANKET SHARING HIS BED WITH HIS EPHEMERA THE FIRST NIGHT

FADE OUT.

BENJAMIN FRANKLINS APPRENTICES

January 1778 the print shop room in Benjamin Franklin's offices in Philadelphia are active with assiduous apprentices aiding in the daily grind. Ravishing 17 year olds Trevor and Radcliff are deeply engulfed with another discreetly bussing in the privacy of the print room before an animated Benjamin Franklin unexpectedly comes through the egress catching his racy apprentices in action.

BENJAMIN FRANKLIN

I was just going to ask if you boys were hungry, I see that your busy I shall come back later I hate to interrupt an episode.

Benjamin peacefully closes the door behind him giving his apprentices accord.

BENJAMIN FRANKLIN IN FRANCE NEGOTIATING THE TREATY OF ALLIANCE

FADE OUT.

A DEATH THAT BRINGS PEACE

March 1778 in Boston. A crier arriving on horseback delivers Jacob word of Phillip Burns death and his official volution to relinquish him all his land and entire estate. Elated by Philips disposition he gathers his possessions and says adieu to his best mates. Accosting Zac to join him on the pilgrimage to his new abode they retire from their beloved hometown in direction of Point Pleasant Beach, New Jersey.

JACOB AND ZAC TOURING THE ESTATE, THE GROUNDS, AND THE OCEAN VISTA

After touring all the inherited lands with his dearest Zac, Jacob sends for a messenger to decree invitations to Tobias, Sebastian, Seymour and Morgan ennobling his proposal to unite with them on the coast, to live out an gourmand lifestyle together. After being routed through the tavern in New York to their present locale, the invitees receive his coquetry and plans to give fete to the opportunity.

SEYMOUR AND MORGAN RECEIVING THE INVITE IN ALBANY AND CELEBRATE WITH ELONGATED KISSES AND CARESS

Seymour abdicating Thaddeus hegemony to the asylum in Albany and granting him a passionate kiss cheerio telling him to come visit soon. Seymour handing him the master key to the cellar stock room and stash. Thaddeus embraces Seymour and Morgan together saying his good-byes.

JACOB AND ZAC ON THEIR PRIVATE BEACH FACING THE OCEAN BEGIN TO MAKE OUT LUSTFULLY.

TOBIAS AND SEBASTIAN RECEIVE INVITATION IN PHILADELPHIA

Days after returning from their winter stint in the encampment with Commander Washington Tobias and Sebastian receive the letter and are ecstatic about the news setting for a same day departure to incorporate with their cheeky pards. Parting their families farewell they submit to Jacobs supplication.

TOBIAS AND SEBASTIAN HUGGING THEIR MOTHERS FAREWELL AS THEIR FAMILIES WISH THEM WELL FADE OUT.

SAILING FOR A DREAM

Todd and Garret standing closely together in the front of their vessel leaning over the railing staring down at the impressive ocean water splitting headboard. Sailing fastly in the fresh evening wind in attempts to cross the Atlantic to begin their dream.

GARRET

I have this feeling we should never have left the colonies.

Suddenly a hard wave jolts the vessel knocking both overboard as the lovers sink deep in the ocean the sailing vessel surging beyond them out of reach. Arising from the turbid water Todd and Garret grab each others bodies in shock as they watch their last hope of catching their boat sail away without them.

TODD AND GARRET HELPLESSLY HOLD EACH OTHER FLOATING TOGETHER FOR THEIR LAST MOMENTS ALIVE

GORDYS DEMISE

After leaving Providence years back to go into hiding from the law and from Nicholas's kin and friends, Gordy the everlasting lardaceous, isolated renegades time is up. Trapped forlorn in a tiny shanty deep in a Warwick, Rhode Island forest Gordy has no escape route from the vengefulness of the clan knocking down his front door.

GORDYS LAST SCREAMS SHRIEK THROUGH THE FOREST MOMENTS BEFORE A BARRAGE OF GUNSHOTS RIDDLE HIS BLUBBERY CARCAS BREATHLESS

FADE TO RED.

DAWNING OF ETERNITY

This six retired bar hands unite in cultism prorating a group hug on the sandy New Jersey shore. Tossing aside their threads in concert they dash stark naked in the surging ocean corkscrews.

THE SIX NAKED SWEETHEARTS SPLASHING IN THE OCEAN TIDE

Nothing but love and eternity swims in their minds.

FADE OUT.

TIME FOR ENLISTMENT

Gerard, Bobby, and Billy stare at each other with pride as they wait to be officially enlisted in the ranks of the American army in Raleigh. Jonah and Drake enlist together joining the overmountain men in western Kentucky. One armed Christopher enlists. Brad and Paul enlist together. Spencer and Jeff enlist together. Dawson and Timmy enlist together. Elijah and Justin join Washington's men.

THE END
CREDITS

SEYMOUR
MORGAN
TOBIAS
SEBASTIAN
ZAC
JACOB
GORDON
THADDEUS
GERARD
BILLY
BOBBY
EBAN
JACK
CHARLES
CUDDY
SCOTT
ROBERT
SAMUEL
DR. MATTHEWS
CALVIN
NICHOLAS
PETER
STEPHEN
RICKY
ROGER
DOCKMASTER RYAN
TOBIAS'S FATHER
TOBIAS'S MOTHER
AMELIA
CHRISTOPHER
BAR HAND
DRUNK GUY
MRS. FRANK
BARTENDER
ABE
CY

JOSH
TERRY
SPENCER
JEFF
TODD
GARRET
BRAD
PAUL
TIMMY
TAYLOR
GORDONS FATHER
GORDONS MOTHER
DENNY
HARRY
CYRUS
JAMIE
DON
NAKED MAN 1
NAKED MAN 2
THE BOY DAWSON
TIMMY
SISTER 1
SISTER 2
DANIEL
SETH
CHARLES
CRAIG
STANLEY
JUSTIN
ELIJAH
ELIAS
DRAKE
JONAH
CHEROKEE INDIAN
CORY
LTNT. DUDLINSON
PATRICK HENRY
JOHN JAY
SAMUEL ADAMS
JOHN ADAMS
JOHN HANCOCK
PAUL REVERE

NATHAN HALE
ROBERT MORRIS
BENJAMIN FRANKLIN
GEORGE WASHINGTON

AFTER CREDITS SCENE

Plump in parody Robert Morris arises from on all fours from under the hoarded dinner table slowly to his feet. As Ronnie and the two raffish visiting orphans burst hysterically at their daddy for the evening.

Contact – Ryan Oeters/facebook.com – or –RyanOeters.com questions, comments or to purchase the script for production.